Praise for *From Foresight to Action*

Given the increasing importance of navigating uncertainty by influencing the future, many professionals are focusing on Foresight. I have yet to meet one that exhibits the passion, affinity, and commitment that Joana has; she has become an ambassador for this approach, adding tremendous value.

Hernan Estrada
Former General Manager, Brazil, The Walt Disney Company
Former SVP Strategy & Business Development, EMEA, The Walt Disney Company

Joana combines her years of experience as a strategist at Disney with her love of Foresight in this unique 'what-if' approach to a business book. Our uncertain times require us to develop the ability to think in simultaneous multiple futures, and Joana's book will equip you to do just that.

Yvette Montero Salvatico
Co-Founder and Managing Director, TFSX

Foresight is quickly becoming one of the essential skills of the future. This book is for readers proactively preparing themselves and their organizations for the new world on the horizon. The ability to think strategically and act with Foresight can be learned, and this book is a vital, practical guide.

Alexandra Whittington
Top 50 Leading Female Futurist

Joana's book unpacks the forces shaping our world and the choices defining what comes next. When shared futures feel uncertain and surreal, Joana offers a business-critical perspective that is thoughtful and urgently needed, challenging us to engage with the future more consciously and creatively.

Trish Long
Former Vice President & General Manager (Ireland), The Walt Disney Studios
Chair, Dublin International Film Festival
Chair, MediCinema Ireland

Joana brings deep experience in applying foresight to strategic decision-making. This book is a practical guide based on real experience, blending theory with clear examples to make futures actionable.

Maria Åkerlund
Strategic Foresight Leader, Inter IKEA Group

I had the pleasure of working with Joana as we built strategic foresight capabilities at The Walt Disney Company. She was a driving force in growing the practice. This book draws on her deep experience to help others bring strategy to life through foresight.

Richard Ramsey
VP Human Resources/Global Futures Team Lead,
Walt Disney International (Retired)

FROM FORESIGHT TO ACTION

FROM FORESIGHT TO ACTION

YOUR STRATEGIC DECISION-MAKING PLAYBOOK

JOANA LENKOVA

WILEY

This edition first published 2026

Registered Offices
John Wiley & Sons, Inc., 111 River Street, Hoboken, NJ 07030, USA
John Wiley & Sons Ltd, New Era House, 8 Oldlands Way, Bognor Regis, West Sussex, PO22 9NQ, UK

For details of our global editorial offices, customer services, and more information about Wiley products visit us at www.wiley.com.

The manufacturer's authorized representative according to the EU General Product Safety Regulation is Wiley-VCH GmbH, Boschstr. 12, 69469 Weinheim, Germany, e-mail: Product_Safety@wiley.com.

Wiley also publishes its books in a variety of electronic formats and by print-on-demand. Some content that appears in standard print versions of this book may not be available in other formats.

Library of Congress Cataloging-in-Publication Data
Names: Lenkova, Joana author
Title: From foresight to action : your strategic decision-making playbook / Joana Lenkova.
Description: Hoboken, NJ : John Wiley & Sons, Inc, [2026] | Includes bibliographical references and index.
Identifiers: LCCN 2026017997 | ISBN 9781394425884 hardback | ISBN 9781394425907 adobe pdf | ISBN 9781394425891 epub
Subjects: LCSH: Decision making
Classification: LCC HD30.23 .I457 2026
LC record available at https://lccn.loc.gov/2026017997

Cover Design: Wilmarie Deetlefs
Cover Image Design: Courtesy of Wilmarie Deetlefs
Author Photo: Courtesy of Joana Lenkova

Set in 11/14.5pt BemboStd by Lumina Datamatics

Printed and bound by CPI Group (UK) Ltd, Croydon, CR0 4YY

C9781394425884_030726

Limited use of AI tools supported the identification of relevant and contemporary literature and citation formatting. All intellectual content, tools, analysis, and conclusions remain the author's own and represent her views and expertise.

For those bold enough to choose their own path to better futures.

Contents

Foreword

This is not an easy time for humanity. We see this at the external level in the conflicts, the supply chain disruptions, the pandemics and the palpable fear around shifts in global power. But this is also true at the inner level. I recall a CEO who came to me feeling a deep anxiety about the future. He no longer knew what to expect; the future felt not just uncertain, but deeply fearful.

We worked through an inner process, a journey to create a new story for him. He went from being a person who could only play on one type of tennis court, with one strategy for one expected world, to someone who could play on many different courts. He had begun the process of futures-proofing himself, of preparing for alternatives. As we went deeper into his life narrative, he had a realization. 'This was never about the game', he said, 'not the money or even the tennis analogy. It was always about the joy of hitting the ball, the simple focus of it'. From there, he shifted his long-term narrative to 'the rally' — the mindfulness of being present in the moment. In this way, futures work, as Joana Lenkova teaches us, is never just about prediction. It is about preparedness, at both the external and the inner levels.

The beauty of Joana Lenkova's book is that she shares her authentic experiences, from various multinational organizations, and her conclusions are both simple and powerful. She reminds us that small steps forward are still progress, that not everyone needs to be a futurist to do better strategy. What truly matters is intentional and meaningful integration.

This last part is critical. In my own 45-year journey through futures studies, I have seen that foresight works best not as a checklist or a search for a magical solution, but as Lenkova says, as a purposeful integration into the deep narrative of an organization. Without that, the work may look good on the surface, but it won't prepare you for the inevitable shocks that will come, and keep on coming.

And this is where this book shines: its authenticity. It is written from a place of truth. You can feel the future changing around you, and without the language of foresight, you won't be able to express this feeling in a way that the Head of HR, or Finance, or the Board Chair will understand. Like our CEO, futures thinking gives you new skills to navigate a world that feels uncertain and chaotic.

But Lenkova takes us a step further. She writes that once you have the skills, you have a responsibility to decide. She helps us choose wisely, to reduce the space between 'knowing and doing, between foresight and action, between futures intelligence and resilient future strategy'.

This takes time, of course. The gap may never fully disappear, as novel shocks will always emerge to challenge how we see the world. Yet, slowly, we enhance our ability to use the future, to pick up on emerging issues and weak signals, and to understand what is merely noise and what is a profound shift.

This book is a guide in that endeavour. It is written as a playbook, easy to follow with the clear intent that you start your own foresight journey today.

Lenkova leaves the toughest challenge for last. She asks, 'When the future challenges your assumptions, will you protect what exists or design what comes next?'

For me, the answer is clear. The entire world system, the very health of our planet, depends on our courage to design what's next — not just by learning new skills, but by becoming new ourselves.

Professor Sohail Inayatullah
UNESCO Chair in Futures Studies, Professor at
Tamkang University and Researcher at Metafuture

Preface: A Futurist's Journey

Clearing the Front Window

In 2015, I joined The Walt Disney Company in a strategy role based in the United Kingdom for Disneyland Paris.

For generations of families around the world, Disneyland represents imagination made tangible. It's a place where stories step into reality, a magical world that comes alive. Contributing to the stewardship of that brand meant operating at the intersection of commercial performance and cultural meaning.

I defined the strategic direction for consumer growth across the UK and Ireland and assessed additional emerging territories to understand where future demand might develop beyond these established markets. Part of my mandate was dedicated to identifying what I came to think of as the 'markets of the future'. That meant analysing things like demographic momentum, economic signals, travel accessibility, and cultural affinity to determine which regions could become meaningful engines of growth over time. That responsibility demanded simultaneous focus: delivering against present targets while anticipating structural changes shaping demand ahead. Managing both established markets and emerging territories brought its own challenges given that both had different time horizons, certainty levels and measures of success.

The analytical environment was rigorous. Anyone entering a big corporate sooner rather than later meets head to head with the multiple sources of internal performance data. Forecast models, segmentation frameworks, booking patterns, elasticity assumptions ... every lever was scrutinized. Yet, I became increasingly aware that fluctuations in demand were often influenced by forces our internal performance frameworks were not explicitly designed to track.

External forces were reshaping the landscape in ways no quarterly model could fully anticipate. Travel disruptions linked to the migrant crisis were affecting key rail routes from the UK to continental Europe. The November 2015 attacks in Paris shifted travel sentiment almost overnight, particularly for families. The announcement of the UK's EU referendum introduced sustained political and economic uncertainty, and currency fluctuations began influencing discretionary spending decisions in very tangible ways.

Each of these developments sat outside of our control and outside our data. Yet each of them influenced performance in ways that no internal dashboard could fully explain in isolation.

Leading consumer growth in that environment required more than reactive adjustments. It required the ability to widen the lens to examine not only conversion rates and campaign effectiveness, but also structural signals emerging across society, politics, infrastructure and economics. I began to recognize that while our internal systems were sophisticated, they were primarily designed to optimize within existing conditions and I wasn't looking in the right place for the answers I needed. I wasn't asking the right question to begin with and that realization stayed with me.

It sparked a deeper curiosity about how large organizations could deliberately design for uncertainty, rather than merely respond to it. I already knew about scenario planning and how Royal Dutch Shell used it successfully. I had the mindset, but I didn't yet have the tools and skills to operate in that realm. I was eager to learn a disciplined way to monitor the outside world, interpret weak signals early and incorporate them into growth decisions before they translated into volatility on a balance sheet.

Soon after this realization, I was selected to join the company's Futures initiatives and was trained by Frank Spencer and Yvette Montero Salvatico from The Futures School — professionals with a history of foresight research and corporate experience. In fact, Yvette previously worked for TWDC for

13 years, eventually leading Future Workforce Insights within Walt Disney Parks and Resorts.

Their work introduced structure to what had until then been instinct. Foresight is not about prediction; it is about preparedness. It provided practical tools to identify emerging patterns, construct plausible scenarios and stress-test strategic assumptions before they hardened into commitments.

I remember the first workshop vividly. I sat in the front row, completely absorbed. There was a clarity in the way Frank articulated complexity that made everything click. I felt energized, not because I had discovered something entirely new, but because I had found the language and tools for a mindset I had already been living by. It felt like cleaning the front window of a fast-moving vehicle. The road ahead had always been there. Now I could simply see it more clearly and I had this zest for life. I wanted to use this spark to make positive changes inside and beyond boardrooms.

It didn't take long for me to realize that foresight was not an abstract intellectual exercise. It was deeply practical, because it changed how conversations were framed, how risks were evaluated, and how investment timing was considered. It encouraged us to ask a different question. Not 'What are we optimizing for?' but 'Under which future conditions does this decision still hold?'

I became increasingly involved in advancing futures work alongside my consumer strategy responsibilities. What had started as curiosity evolved into commitment. I could see that the organizations best positioned for resilience were not necessarily those with the best data. They were those that could interpret change early and adapt deliberately.

Around the same time, I enrolled in the Strategy and Innovation postgraduate programme at Saïd Business School, University of Oxford. My research focused on how strategic foresight could create a better marketplace positioning for established organizations navigating volatility and ensure they remain flexible under the pressures of the operating environment. The narrative then was that start-ups are agile and able to innovate and disrupt. My hypothesis was that if legacy companies could balance exploitation of current resources with exploration of new opportunities, they were actually in a more favourable position to disrupt. The academic frameworks sharpened the practice and the corporate environment tested it under pressure.

By 2019, foresight had moved from an additional skill to a central focus of my work and my passion. I left my amazing team and job at The Walt Disney Company to follow my dream path of becoming the best futurist I can be. This was when I founded Futures Forward in London. I wanted to apply what I had learned across different sectors — corporations, but also public institutions and NGOs — to understand how decision systems respond to uncertainty. I have always aimed to combine the creativity that foresight provides me with the tangibility that business requires, so that became my niche.

Across contexts, I observed the same pattern. Leaders acknowledged disruption, they commissioned reports, hosted innovation sessions. But translating foresight into specific, sometimes uncomfortable, strategic decisions proved far more challenging than generating ideas.

In 2021, I stepped into the role of Futurology Director at The LEGO Group — a role that embedded foresight directly within corporate innovation. Few organizations at the time had a dedicated futurist in residence. The global pandemic had accelerated awareness of systemic fragility, but awareness alone does not redesign processes. Skillful and meaningful integration does.

Over the past decade, practicing foresight within commercially accountable environments has clarified something for me: the barrier is rarely intelligence or access to information. It is courage and structure. The courage to confront signals that may disrupt today's success. The ***structure*** to translate those signals into decisions ***before*** certainty arrives.

And this is why I wrote this book. I am not here to predict the future, nor am I here to romanticize it. But I have gained experience that others have found valuable. Foresight practitioners in large corporations who are a few years behind me in their journeys have sought me out for guidance and I have willingly provided it. Now I am here to share my experience with you, hoping that you will take my learnings and develop your own, even better, ways to navigate the future.

In the 10 years I've worked with corporate foresight, I have learned a few things. I am here to share these learnings with you.

- If you want progress, you sometimes have to break the rules and hack the tools.
- Small steps forward are still progress.

- Not everyone has to drink the Kool-Aid.
- Not everyone needs to be a futurist to do better strategy.
- What really matters is intentional and meaningful integration.

Because when foresight lives on the side as a workshop, a report, or an intellectual exercise, it rarely changes decisions. When it becomes overly theoretical, it kills the vibe and no action follows.

You do not need to become a professional futurist to think more effectively about the future (*though you probably shouldn't call yourself one if you are not trained and practicing — the futures community really dislikes that*). What you need are tools that connect weak signals to real strategy, uncertainty to investment decisions and foresight to commitment.

This book is my attempt to bridge that gap, to make foresight practical, embedded and decision-oriented.

Because the future does not wait until we are certain and feel ready.

And the organizations that thrive are not the ones who forecast perfectly. They are the ones who prepare deliberately.

So here it is. My experience, my approach, and my thinking. I hope you follow my advice to take these tools and modify them, make them your own and evolve the practice so we can get closer to making the futures practice work in organizations.

And because strategy is rarely linear and I always thought, why follow the conventional path, I made this into a Choose-Your-Own-Path book. You can start where the tension is and begin making some decisions about your future.

Happy reading,
Joana

Acknowledgements

Nothing meaningful we achieve is done alone. Although this work carries my name, it would not have been possible without the many people who have been part of my journey. I often reflect on the conversations, experiences and moments of guidance that shape how we see the world. Every interaction — whether encouraging, challenging, thought-provoking, or sometimes even limiting — has something to teach us, and I am deeply grateful for the many mentors and influences I have encountered along the way.

First and foremost, to my incredible family. Thank you for your love, your patience and your unwavering belief in me. Your support has sustained me throughout this journey more than words can truly express. Kaloyan, my brother, who is one of my biggest cheerleaders. Dad, I know you would have been proud. And to my mom, whose immense bravery, exceptional personal example, and loving encouragement have always meant more than I can fully say.

To my wonderful friends, I am so lucky to share this journey with you. To my futures peers, and to the many people who have shared their time, ideas, and conversations with me over the years — thank you. Your perspectives, support and curiosity have enriched both my life and my work.

To the many clients and collaborators I have had the privilege of working with over the years — thank you for your trust, your openness, and your willingness to explore new opportunities together.

I am especially grateful to my Futures teachers, Frank and Yvette, who first ignited the spark in me that led to a career change that ultimately brought me here. My sincere thanks also go to my leaders, and mentors, especially those at The Walt Disney Company, where my futures journey began — especially Peter Welch, Hernan Estrada, Trish Long, Richard Ramsey and the Futures team at The Walt Disney Company, whose imagination and generosity of thought were a constant source of inspiration. Thanks also go to internationally-respected futurist Professor Sohail Inayatullah for generously writing the Foreword for this book and Professor René Rohrbeck for his research in corporate foresight, proving its value.

To my professors and mentors at Saïd Business School at the University of Oxford, especially Professor Marc Ventresca and Professor Rafael Ramirez, as well as my classmates, many of whom have become lifelong friends and business partners, you continue to inspire me every single day. Your curiosity, insight and commitment to exploring new ideas challenge me to think more deeply about the futures we are shaping together.

To the people who believed in me and this book when it was just an idea — Georgia Psyllidou, Daniel Tate, Ivan Ilieff, Alex Whittington, Melissa Noonan, Sarah Owen, Ellie Moore, Alex Eley, Frederic Caufrier, Teodora and Martin Arvidsson, Tracey Dynan, Vid Veerapen, Antony Atanasov, Chris Danusiar, to Wilmarie Deetlefs — thank you for the beautiful designs, they gave the book its visual life, and the many others who pre-ordered copies before a single page was written. Thank you for your belief and your patience. I hope it was worth the wait.

To Kelly Vero, who reminded me that I had something worth saying and gave me the final push to finish this book.

To my amazing agent, Chris Newson, for believing in this work and helping guide it into the world.

To my editor, Annie Knight, who saw the potential in this book and brought me on board with enthusiasm and belief in the idea. To Stacey Rivera and Alice Hadaway for their thoughtful guidance and care throughout the editorial, production and publication process.

And to Georgia Kirke and team — thank you for your insight, patience, and craft. I have learned so much from working with you.

To my publisher, Wiley, for giving this book a home and the opportunity to share these ideas with readers everywhere.

The futures are shaped by the people we learn from, the conversations we have, and the ideas we choose to pursue. The rest is up to us — to imagine and to choose our own path forward.

Introduction

You Are Already in the Future

The future doesn't come with a big announcement. There are no alarm bells. There is no dramatic turning point, no moment when the room suddenly goes dark and someone says, 'This changes everything'. You're not on a strategy offsite or in a boardroom listening to a groundbreaking presentation by a team of highly paid consultants. There might not even be a crisis.

The moment you realize the future is here usually happens in a very ordinary Tuesday morning catch-up meeting. A colleague mentions a competitor you didn't know existed. Someone shares a viral video that suddenly explains a shift you hadn't been able to name. A behaviour change shows up quietly in your core customer group, right after a strong quarterly result. Maybe a new technology launches faster than expected or a regulation that seemed distant two months ago is now a hard constraint on how you operate.

Nobody stops talking, but a kind of heavy silence settles in the room. You feel it … the tension rising. You realize the future has arrived faster than this organization's ability to process it, let alone respond to it.

There was no dramatic disruption you can point to and no single wild card you can blame. Just a subtle signal that lands in your gut: 'we should have been better prepared to withstand the pressure of this turn of events'.

This feeling is familiar to most leaders. How they deal with it is unique to each one of them. Some ignore it, others bury it beneath good results and full calendars. This tension fades as they get pulled back into more meetings, more dashboards, more reports, more short-term decisions that feel urgent but strangely disconnected. And it is somehow comforting not having to think about the big monster and deal with the little issues at hand. We're ticking off boxes — 'done!' one small problem at a time. All the while, the bigger one is looming over you and maybe even growing.

Very few pause long enough to name what is actually happening: uncertainty making itself visible, creeping into the operating space one signal at a time.

We often tell ourselves that the pace of change has accelerated, that the future is arriving faster than ever before. In response, we collect information. We commission trend reports. Some organizations build scenarios. Others hire futurists.

And yet, it is surprisingly easy to feel overwhelmed rather than empowered. We accumulate knowledge about what might happen, without knowing how to use it in ways that genuinely shape decisions. The question quietly shifts from, 'What's coming?' to something more uncomfortable:

So what?

So what if I know the top 10 trends for the next five years? So what if I can describe multiple plausible futures? How does any of this actually change what I decide to do — today, tomorrow, next quarter?

The real question is not whether the future is moving towards you at speed. It is what you do in the moment when you realize it has already arrived.

Why Strategies Break Under Uncertainty

For most of the last century, strategy was built on a relatively stable assumption: that the world moved in something close to straight lines. The dominant logic of strategic planning emerged in a post-war context where markets were more predictable, growth was often linear and the future could be treated as an extension of the recent past.

Strategy, in that world, meant drawing a single line into the future and doing everything possible to stay on it.

Seen from today, this approach can feel naïve. But at the time, it often worked. Data was well-behaved, the patterns repeated and the forecasts felt reliable.

However, that world is now long gone.

Today's environment is better described by what some call transience and polycrisis: multiple overlapping disruptions whose interactions are non-linear, compounding and difficult to model. Risks no longer arrive in isolation, but cascade across systems. The World Economic Forum (WEF) notes that risk has become networked, cascading and compounding.[1] These global risks are increasingly interconnected and capable of producing cascading impacts across systems. Climate, geopolitics, technology, culture and economics clash and evolve together, shaping and amplifying one another in ways no single actor controls.

If we know all this, if we talk openly about uncertainty and complexity, why do so many organizations still plan as if producing more spreadsheets will restore their sense of control?

Part of the answer lies not in strategy itself, but in how we have been trained to think. Culturally, professionally and educationally, we are taught to expect one right answer. School rewards certainty, then corporate planning reinforces it: one forecast, one roadmap, one officially sanctioned version of the future.

Research consistently shows how fragile this assumption is. Even highly skilled experts struggle to predict beyond very short time horizons, as Philip Tetlock's research on expert political forecasting demonstrated. Analysing tens of thousands of predictions made by political and economic experts, Tetlock found that experts were often only slightly more accurate than chance, particularly for longer-term forecasts.[2] Accuracy declines sharply as uncertainty increases, highlighting the limits of prediction in complex systems.[3]

Sometimes we think the problem is lack of competence. But in fact, it is the mental model we continue to rely on, namely the belief in linearity and control that unfortunately no longer matches the world we operate in.

When a strategy breaks under uncertainty, it is rarely because a leader made a careless decision. It breaks because the logic guiding that decision was designed for a different environment. One where complexity could be simplified away rather than engaged with.

The danger is that this failure often unfolds quietly. It doesn't show up as a sudden collapse, but as a series of small blind spots, misread signals and assumptions that harden into risk. By the time the gap becomes visible, it has usually turned into a business problem … or a crisis.

Holding a single straight line into the future is no longer an asset but a liability. It locks you into one story about how the world will behave and encourages you to ignore anything that does not fit neatly within it.

Today's success does not make tomorrow safer. The problem you are solving right now may not even exist in the future you are moving toward.

So the uncomfortable question becomes: are the precise answers in your strategy decks responding to a world that is already disappearing?

Futures Thinking Is Not Prediction

When I began working in foresight over a decade ago, futures thinking was still a niche practice inside most organizations. In recent years, especially after the pandemic, many have embraced the need for a more outward-looking perspective. Signals, trends and scenarios have become part of the strategic conversation. This book assumes you are already there.

It assumes you understand that the future is not singular, that uncertainty is unavoidable and that waiting for clarity is no longer a viable strategy. It assumes the problem is not a lack of information. The real challenge lies elsewhere.

Futures thinking is often misunderstood as a way to predict what will happen and that's the criteria it's measured against. But in reality, its value lies somewhere else entirely.

It is not, and has never been, about forecasting the future. It is about improving the quality of the decisions you make, when the future cannot be known, as is usually the case.

Uncertainty is not a temporary condition we pass through on the way back to stability. It is the surrounding environment in which we live, operate and conduct business. We can't eliminate it. Instead we have to learn how to work with it without freezing, oversimplifying or defaulting to familiar answers that no longer fit.

The Decision Gap

Across very different organizations — corporates, NGOs and public institutions — I have seen the same pattern repeat.

Teams produce thoughtful foresight work, scenarios are developed, then implications are mapped and presentations follow. The room agrees unanimously: 'yes, this will impact us', and then people leave the room and return to decisions shaped by short-term pressure, existing incentives and familiar ways of working.

At this point, the issue becomes not taking a proactive approach to choosing what to do once you have seen what various futures may look like. In this situation, it is less about not being able to foresee it.

I call this space the Decision Gap. The gap between knowing and doing. Between futures intelligence and future-ready action.

It is where uncertainty overwhelms confidence. Where political friction distorts judgement. Where past success quietly makes change feel dangerous. Where 'wait and see' unfortunately becomes the default response.

This book is written to address this specific gap.

Its purpose is not to help you imagine better futures in theory, but to help you practice making better decisions inside the messy, ambiguous, high-stakes situations you actually face.

Along the way, something else tends to happen. As people work through these decisions, patterns emerge about how they relate to risk, how far into the future they are comfortable committing, and whether they instinctively protect what exists or explore what could be.

This book is as much about noticing how you decide as it is about deciding what to do.

How to Use This Playbook

This is not meant to be read as a textbook, it is a strategic rehearsal space. You can think of it as a flight simulator for decisions under uncertainty.

You can explore possible futures, test different moves and experience the consequences on the page before committing to them in real life. It won't lead you to finding the 'right' answer, instead its value lies in noticing what you prioritize, avoid or delay when certainty is removed from the equation.

There are two ways to move through the book.

1. Follow the full journey. If you read from front to back, the book works as a capability-building arc.

Part I builds the mindset and tools needed to think in multiple futures. Part II places you inside five Strategic Futures Labs, each focused on a real decision leaders face. Part III helps you turn what you have learned into a repeatable, future-ready practice for yourself and your organization.

2. Or start with the question that matters most and choose the Strategic Futures Lab that is most relevant to this question. If you have an urgent issue on your desk, you can begin in the middle.

The heart of the book is five standalone Strategic Futures Labs. Each one is organized around a different strategic question and can be read independently. You can start wherever the pressure feels highest.

Individually, each Lab helps you make clearer choices in one domain. Together, they form an integrated outside-in strategy model: future customer → future product → future opportunity → future innovation → future strategy.

As you move through them, you will gradually build a picture not only of the futures you are preparing for, but of the decision patterns you rely on to get there.

This book is not organized around single-minded answers, but around choices. Because it is choices repeated over time that shape our strategies, organizations and futures.

When we weigh consequences, compare paths or imagine alternatives, we are already 'using the future' to decide in the present. The only question is whether we do it consciously and well.

The Leadership Decisions This Book Helps You Make

Each Lab asks you to make a different kind of decision.

Some clarify what should matter. Others force you to decide what no longer should. Some help you choose where to act, where to wait and where to let go.

You can run any Lab on its own, but be aware that skipping one means skipping that decision, not just skipping content.

Each Strategic Futures Lab in this book is built around a specific leadership question. They are not variations of the same exercise. They ask you to make different kinds of decisions — ones leaders often avoid, postpone or make implicitly without noticing.

The five Labs address the following leadership questions:

- **Lab 1 — Future Human Relevance**
  Where could it plausibly make sense for us to matter in the future — to humans, not just customers? This Lab helps you step outside current markets and categories to understand which human needs are likely to come under pressure — and where relevance might need to be re-earned.

- **Lab 2 — Portfolio Future Relevance**
  Which of our current products or services deserve to be carried forward — and which should no longer anchor our strategy? This is often the most uncomfortable Lab. It asks leaders to distinguish between what performs well today and what remains legitimate tomorrow. The forced choices here are intentional.
- **Lab 3 — External Posture and Risk**
  Which external forces require action, which justify preparation and which do we consciously choose to accept? This Lab turns trend noise into governance clarity by making leadership posture explicit.
- **Lab 4 — Innovation Focus**
  Where is it worth engaging uncertainty through innovation — and where is it not? Rather than generating ideas, this Lab helps leaders decide where exploration deserves attention — and where restraint is the better choice.
- **Lab 5 — Strategy Resilience**
  Will our current strategy still work under plausible future pressure — and what must change to make it resilient? This Lab stress-tests strategic commitments against multiple futures to reveal vulnerabilities before they become crises.

If you are unsure where to begin, start with Lab 1. It establishes the future conditions and human priorities that give meaning to every decision that follows. If you are already facing a specific pressure, you can begin with the Lab that matches the question you are blocked on.

PART I Getting Future Ready

Some of you reading this book may be ready to dive straight into practical exercises, in which case please feel free to skip to Part II and begin tackling the Strategic Futures Labs. However, I imagine some of you reading this are curious, but not yet entirely sold on the value of foresight and futures intelligence.

Perhaps you are still a little unclear on what it is. Or why it is so vital for organizations in the 21st century. The chapters in this first part of the book will not only help you understand its value, but also to see why embedding foresight and futures intelligence into organizations is business critical.

This is where I will make the business case for foresight and begin giving you a shared language you can use to discuss the challenges it throws up with others in your organization.

Before we go further, I'd like to share some terms to help you understand and navigate your futures journey. Throughout this book, I use several related terms: futures thinking, strategic foresight and futures intelligence.

Futures thinking refers to the mindset of considering multiple possible futures rather than assuming the present will continue unchanged.

Strategic foresight is the structured practice of exploring those futures to understand emerging risks, opportunities and shifts that may shape decisions.

Futures intelligence refers to the capability of organizations to continuously detect signals of change, interpret their implications and use that understanding to guide decisions over time.

Part I will help you develop your futures thinking ahead of the practical exercises in Part II.

Here, we'll also explore the Decision Gap in more detail and why, despite having more data available than at any point in history, leadership teams still struggle to make future-focused decisions.

Part III is all about creating a mindset shift, where foresight and futures intelligence are no longer seen as a special function or additional insight provided by an external consultant, but where they are seen as a critical element of business decision-making.

We'll also explore the origins of business strategy to help better understand why we make decisions in the way we do — and to see why existing ways of thinking are no longer fit for the modern era.

First, let's dive into why foresight isn't just a nice to have. It's business critical.

1 The Business-critical Case for Foresight

The quantitative and qualitative business case for foresight. The finance case for foresight. Moving from knowledge to action.

The contemporary business world has entered a period of time defined by structural instability. Yet, the frameworks we use and the way our companies are organized follow the rules of the old world, where volatility was somewhat manageable. Corporate strategy is still built around linear forecasting, looking backwards to extrapolate into the future. We build five-year plans, 'locking' them in place and trusting they will remain resilient for a world that will be characterized by one word 'unpredictable'.

The Decision Gap: Why Knowing Is Not the Same as Acting

There is something deeply misleading about how we talk about strategy today.

We talk about insight, market intelligence, trend awareness, geopolitical risks and dashboards, digital transformation roadmaps … We seem to have so much information at our fingertips. We sound so confident, as though we believe that once we have gathered all of this information, we will have conquered the difficult part. We behave as if knowledge naturally translates into forward movement in the right direction.

But if that were true, organizations would be shifting course and making changes towards better outcomes and opportunities far earlier than they actually do.

The reality is that there is a continuous, deep and costly gap between recognizing that the operating environment and customer needs are shifting and being intentional and willing to commit meaningful resources in response. Or better yet, being able to anticipate potential change from the early signals and proactively preparing the organization for any potential future, maybe even creating the trends. Courageous! But not usual when risk management is at the core of business.

Leaders often see and understand that technology is accelerating, customer expectations are evolving, and regulation will come along and reshape the playing field. They read the reports. They invite experts and attend the briefings. They even discuss the signals in the board meetings. But when the moment comes to reallocate capital away from established revenue streams and toward uncertain futures, deep hesitation sets in.

This is the Decision Gap.

The Decision Gap, as I explained in the Introduction, is the chasm between awareness that the world is changing, even if there's an indication on how it's changing, and a strategic commitment to act upon this information. It is that very uncomfortable space where the data says '*prepare*', but the incentives say '*wait a little longer*'. It is this invisible delay, almost like a slow-motion movie, between recognizing the risk and taking the decision to restructure for resilience.

But in a world that has become increasingly non-linear and very interconnected, that delay starts to compound and the consequences are substantial.

Beyond Forecasting: From Continuity to Discontinuity

For decades, corporate planning relied on forecasting as its central discipline. Forecasting indeed remains indispensable. It allows organizations to manage liquidity, coordinate supply chains, plan workforce requirements and communicate expectations to investors, reassuring them. It extends patterns from the past into the near future and quantifies the probable range of outcomes based on the available data.

But forecasting carries the assumption that underpins its legitimacy: **structural continuity**. It assumes that while volatility may occur, the underlying logic of the system largely remains intact. That assumption has weakened.

We now operate in what many describe as a **BANI** world[1]:

- **Brittle** systems that fracture under stress.
- **Anxious** populations reacting rapidly to uncertainty.
- **Non-linear** dynamics, where small signals trigger disproportionate effects.
- Environments that often feel **incomprehensible** until retrospectively explained.

In such settings, projecting yesterday's numbers forward may optimize execution, but it does not necessarily protect relevance.

Within this context, strategic foresight emerges not as a speculative luxury, but as a critical dynamic capability for large organizations seeking to maintain long-term marketplace positioning and sustainable growth.[2]

It is useful here to differentiate three modes of futures thinking:

1. **Nowcasting** enhances visibility into what is happening in real time. It focuses on estimating the present and the immediate future. The term originated in meteorology and was later adopted in economics to update key indicators using recently published data.[3]
2. **Forecasting** is a quantitative approach that extends current trajectories into the expected near future, usually 3–18 months.
3. **Strategic Foresight** *does not predict.* It is a qualitative, structured approach that explores multiple plausible futures, including those that break from present patterns.

Nowcasting increases situational awareness and sharpens visibility, while allowing leadership teams to understand what is unfolding in real time and to respond **tactically** when volatility appears.

Forecasting improves operational coordination and aligns functions around a shared expectation of what demand, cost or growth is likely to look like in the near future. It brings discipline and creates planning coherence. It is extremely useful, and in many contexts, absolutely necessary.

Strategic Foresight is often measured by the same expectations around certainty and prediction that are applied to forecasting, but it actually operates on a very different layer. It does not predict. Instead, it deliberately explores multiple future scenarios and pathways. Strategic foresight expands strategic imagination before disruption makes adaptation delayed and reactive, because it looks at possibilities that fall outside the logic of extension. It exists to stretch the leadership team's thinking beyond what is statistically probable in the short-term toward what is structurally plausible in the long-term.

None of these approaches replaces the others, and it would be irresponsible to suggest that organizations abandon forecasting. The problem appears when predictive forecasting becomes the dominant, and very often the only, logic used in environments where structural disruptions are not rare anomalies, but a repeating feature of reality.

Forecasts are very powerful as long as the rules remain stable and the environment predictable and similar to what it was historically. But how often is this the case nowadays?

Strategic foresight asks a different category of question. It asks: what if the rules themselves evolve? What if customer behaviour shifts not a little bit, but fundamentally? What if regulation reshapes the business model of the company or the whole industry?

The main tension in the boardroom is this: leaders are conditioned to ask for certainty. This is how our world has operated and this is how we are taught in school. Capital allocation *feels* safer when tied to quantifiable projections. Shareholders and therefore boards expect clarity, not speculation. And that is why forecasting becomes the preferred tool, because it *appears* to offer controllability. But feels and appears are the right terms here. Because they mask the truth, which is that in BANI environments this excessive reliance on predictive certainty has severe downsides. It blindsides. It delays capital reallocation or focus shift until the signal is statistically undeniable, which usually translates to, 'We are late and now we have to react in panic'. This narrows the options and in fact makes leadership less in control of the outcomes.

Strategic foresight is often misunderstood precisely because of this expectation. It is evaluated by the wrong deliverable. It is expected to provide certainty about the future, as if it were an advanced forecasting instrument.

When it does not produce a single definitive answer, it is perceived as vague. But certainty is not the role of this methodology.

Its role is to widen the frame of consideration before irreversible commitments are made, to explore multiple plausible trajectories rather than defend one assumed continuation, and to make uncertainty visible while there is still room to manoeuvre. Yes, strategic foresight is used for long-term planning, but in my experience adopting the mindset and being actively attuned to the signals the environment sends makes the organization flexible and able to capture not only big future opportunities but also more subtle ones that can be acted on immediately. As long as a decision is taken to act.

Think of it this way: if forecasting protects efficiency within an expected path, strategic foresight protects the organization when the path shifts.

The Quantitative and Qualitative Business Case for Foresight

This C-suite skepticism toward strategic foresight is often encountered, because of the perception that the discipline lacks the financial rigour of traditional planning. Strategic foresight can sound speculative, abstract and difficult to quantify. However, the empirical research is surprisingly robust and indicates that foresight is perhaps the most powerful predictor of long-term outperformance and superior profitability.

The longitudinal study conducted by René Rohrbeck and Ménès Etingue Kum examined 83 multinational firms over a seven-year period (2008–2015) tracking the relationship between 'future preparedness' and financial outcomes. They assessed what they defined as 'Corporate Foresight Maturity'— the structured ability to perceive environmental change, interpret its implications and integrate responses into strategic decision-making.[4]

Their findings were significant.

Companies with high foresight maturity demonstrated approximately 33% higher long-term profitability relative to industry averages. Even more striking, their market capitalization growth exceeded peers by up to 200% over the observed period.

These figures do not mean that future-prepared companies are able to predict events more accurately. They rather suggest that firms capable of systematically engaging with uncertainty position themselves earlier and exit declining paths faster. Preparedness enables timely reallocation and that also compounds.

Performance metric	Future-prepared firms	Performance delta
Long-term profitability	+33% higher than industry average	The 'Foresight Premium'[5]
Market capitalization growth	+200% higher than industry average	Reflecting long-term investor confidence[6]
Probability of outperformance	Significantly higher	Likelihood of becoming an industry leader[7]

The financial logic here is straightforward: firms that accurately interpret the disruptive potential of weak signals and identify emerging opportunities before consensus forms, can reposition their assets and innovation pipeline years before a threat becomes a material liability. This proactive sensing allows companies to capitalize on the 'first-mover' advantages and capture emerging opportunities, while avoiding the 'sunk-cost traps' of industries in decline. And for someone like the Chief Financial Officer of a company, this represents a fundamental shift in how we understand the value of strategic investments.

This means that instead of judging an investment only by the projected return in one projected future, the CFO begins to consider how that investment performs across several possible futures. Instead of asking what is the most likely outcome, we therefore ask a different question, the answer to which feels a lot more strategically important for an organization: 'how exposed are we if the future unfolds differently than planned?'

In simpler terms, it means recognizing that the value of a strategic move is not only in its upside if everything goes according to plan, but also in how much risk it protects us from if things do not.

The expected value of a foresight-driven strategy (EV_{fs}) can be modeled as the sum of the value of strategic options (V_{so}) and the reduction in potential losses from unforeseen threats (L_{ut}), minus the cost of the foresight function (C_{fs})[8]:

$$EV_{fs} = \sum(V_{so} + L_{ut}) - C_{fs}$$

Given that V_{so} includes the 33% profitability bonus and L_{ut} accounts for the avoidance of 'black swan' collapses, the ROI of a foresight function consistently outperforms the cost of its implementation.

The Qualitative Mandate: The Cost of Reinforcing Yesterday

Large organizations rarely become obsolete because they lack intelligence. Beyond the spreadsheets, foresight addresses the qualitative organizational failures, where companies often suffer from an inherent 'corporate blindness' caused by a reinforcement of the very logic that made the organization successful in the past.[9] Historical success shapes metrics. Metrics shape incentives. Incentives shape resource allocation. Over time, this produces path dependency — the tendency of a firm to continue on a trajectory because of historical momentum, even when the environment has shifted. It's a trajectory that feels rational and safe precisely because it has worked before.

When the environment is stable, path dependency is very efficient, but in our current reality, it creates blind spots.

The role of strategic foresight is to shine a light on these blind spots. In doing so, it allows organizations to intervene before the erosion becomes structural, urgent and operationally painful.

Without ensuring this type of thinking is present in a leadership team's portfolio of skills, companies unintentionally continue to sharpen the same sensors that detect yesterday's patterns and ignore tomorrow's changes. They lack the methods and mindset necessary for strategic excellence and resilience.

Strategic foresight breaks this dependency by focusing on the peripheral signals. These are signals that are not in the immediate vicinity of the firm's core industry, but as we know disruptions, as well as innovation, rarely come from inside the industry.

Qualitative benefit	**Mechanism of impact**	**Organizational outcome**
Enhanced perception	Scanning for weak signals outside core markets.[10]	Detection of disruptions before they have a material impact.[11]
Interpretation	Turning raw data into 'futures intelligence'.[12]	Collective understanding of the 'so what' of emerging trends.[13]
Strategic agility	Testing current business models against diverse scenarios.[14]	Ability to pivot rapidly when external conditions change.[15]
Organizational learning	Cross-functional participation in foresight labs.[16]	Breaking silos and fostering a culture of innovation.[17]

More than that though, foresight is also a fantastic tool to 'influence other actors'.[18]

A firm that can articulate a clear, inspirational, well-researched vision of the future can create its desirable future. It can shape the regulatory environment, set industry standards and define customer expectations, effectively creating the very future it is prepared to dominate.

The people who introduced me to foresight — Frank Spencer and Yvette Montero-Salvatico from TFSX — always say, 'Don't wait for the future to happen to you, create it'. Strategic foresight gives you that power.

Addressing the Sceptical CFO: The Finance Case for Foresight

The notion that strategic foresight belongs to innovation teams or strategy units is outdated and needs to be put to bed.

For many CFOs, the hesitation around foresight is not philosophical, it is practical actually and it stems from the perceived lack of certainty. Traditionally, Financial Planning and Analysis (FP&A) is designed to create coherence, minimize variance, align assumptions and deliver what is often referred to as 'single source of truth' to the board. Foresight, conversely, seeks to expand the decision space by acknowledging multiple plausible futures.[19] But plurality can feel dangerous in this context and the multiple futures can look like multiple assumptions, which can feel like diluted accountability.

The 'Silent Killer': A Lack of Strategic Thinking in Finance

Research indicates that the absence of strategic thinking within the finance function can be a 'silent killer' of organizational value.[20] When financial leadership is focused exclusively on short-term quarterly metrics, it is entirely rational to prioritize predictable gains and incremental efficiency improvements. But when structural shifts are happening, this short-term orientation can lead to the deprioritization of long-term growth, resource misallocation and financial instability when the market inevitably shifts.

The issue is that the systems within which the CFO operates reward short-term certainty a lot more visibly than long-term positioning, so naturally this is where the priority lies if choices have to be made. Over time, this leads to reallocation of resources, not because the CFO is conservative, but because uncertainty is treated as a flaw in analysis, rather than a condition that exists when you operate in complex markets.

Strategic foresight invites the CFO and the rest of the leadership team into a different role. Not as those who gatekeep against risk, but as sparring partners to the CEO.[21] By adopting this futurist mindset, the CFO moves from being a 'blocker' of innovative ideas, due to lack of precedent, to someone who co-creates the future of the company. In this role, the CFO ensures the capital allocation is resilient across multiple scenarios, assumptions are stress-tested and investments are structured with learning checkpoints versus locked into rigid parameters.[22]

Transforming FP&A: From Forecasting to Foresight

At this point the distinction between forecasting and foresight is clear. Let's look at what changes inside financial planning when foresight becomes part of the equation.

For the CFO, integrating foresight into capital planning does not mean abandoning rigour, nor does it mean relaxing performance discipline. It simply means acknowledging that major strategic investments — like those in new technologies, platform shifts, infrastructure or acquisitions — will rarely be exposed to a single trajectory. These investments will be positioned in environments that may evolve in substantially different directions.

Traditional capital evaluation is often based on one central projection: a base case that drives discounted cash flow models, valuation assumptions and risk-adjusted returns. Sensitivity analysis typically varies the input parameters like cost, demand and margins, all within that base logic.

Strategic foresight is here to add another layer.

It invites finance to examine whether the underlying logic itself could shift.

When investments are 'wind-tunneled' (see Chapter 8: Lab 5) against diverse future environments, their risk exposure becomes visible but redesign is still possible. The goal is not to prove which future is correct, but to test how robust the decisions remain across the variations. By doing that, the likelihood of overcommitting to a single wrong assumption is significantly reduced. Of course, we can't guarantee protection from volatility and disruption, nobody and no tool can do that for you, but the risk is dramatically decreased.

It ensures that the 'roof is repaired while the sun is shining', rather than during the storm.[23]

In BANI dynamics, the question 'How resilient is this move if conditions diverge from our projection?' is often far more decisive for long-term value creation than asking 'What is the most likely outcome?', which focuses on the precision of a single forecast.

Metric	Traditional forecasting (FP&A)	Strategic foresight
Goal	Accuracy in predicting a single outcome.	Resilience across multiple plausible worlds.
Logic	Linear extrapolation of historical data.	Structured exploration of discontinuous change.
Time horizon	Short to medium-term (1–3 years).	Long-term (5–20+ years).
View of uncertainty	Something to be eliminated.	Something to be embraced as an advantage.

Case Studies in Action: When Foresight Shapes Action

The statistical relationship identified by Rohrbeck and Kum[24] becomes meaningful only when it influences real decisions. Let's explore what that looks like in practice with a few examples.

Novo Nordisk: Capital Committed Before Market Consensus

Novo Nordisk invested heavily in GLP-1 research well before obesity treatment became one of the most commercially significant therapeutic categories globally.[25]

At the time, the company's core diabetes franchise could have justified continuing to concentrate on established revenue streams. Instead, the leadership team expanded its long-term lens, incorporating broader metabolic health trends and demographic developments into capital allocation decisions.

When demand for GLP-1 therapies accelerated, the company did not need to reallocate under pressure. The capabilities and regulatory pathways were already in place.

This proactive shift secured a leading market position and delivered significant shareholder returns, demonstrating that foresight is the engine of 'first-mover' advantage in healthcare.

Siemens: Linking Long-term Exploration to R&D Priorities

Through its 'Pictures of the Future' (PoF) initiative, Siemens structured a cross-functional exploration of emerging developments in infrastructure, energy systems and digital technologies.

What made this meaningful was governance integration. Outputs from PoF informed technology roadmaps and research budgets, influencing which capabilities were developed years before market demand fully crystallized.

In long investment cycles, the timing of capability building determines whether a firm competes from strength or from catch-up.

Royal Dutch Shell: Structural Stress-testing of Major Investments

Shell has utilized scenario planning for over 50 years to examine the implications of geopolitical shifts, regulatory transformation and changes in global energy demand. It also uses scenario planning to challenge executive assumptions.

For Shell, scenarios are not business plans but 'flight simulators' for the mind, intended to push leadership to consider events that may only be remotely possible. By modeling both 'Normative Scenarios' (starting from a goal, like net-zero by 2050) and 'Explorative Scenarios' (starting from current data), Shell ensures that its long-term capital investments in energy infrastructure are resilient to geopolitical tensions and technological shifts like AI-driven energy demand.[26]

The IKEA Experience: The CFO as Agent of Change

During his tenure as CFO of IKEA Poland, Peter Thommen used strategic foresight to navigate a period of massive economic transformation.

By moving beyond spreadsheets and collaborating with futurists from the Copenhagen Institute for Futures Studies, Thommen transformed the finance role at IKEA into one that 'owned the planning process' and served as the 'economic conscience' of the leadership team. This approach allowed IKEA to flourish in a chaotic environment where traditional forecasting was impossible.

Across these examples, the pattern is consistent. Foresight is not an abstract analytical exercise. It is a mechanism that influences when and how capital moves.

That behavioural difference — committing earlier, reallocating sooner, stress-testing assumptions before exposure becomes irreversible — is what ultimately explains the performance differentials identified in longitudinal studies.[27]

The Decision Gap: Bridging Intelligence and Action

By now the business case for strategic foresight should be clear.

A future-ready organization, what some call a 'living company',[28] does not wait for stability to appear or return, because even if it does, stability won't look like we remember it. This type of organization treats uncertainty as a condition of operating, as a truth that is an inherent part of life instead of a temporary situation to be endured. In a BANI world, foresight is about strengthening how decisions are made when multiple futures are plausible. It expands the leadership horizon, strengthens internal dialogue and builds what researchers describe as futures knowledge — a shared understanding of alternative trajectories that shapes present-day allocation.

The chapters that follow move from business case to lived practice. You will not just read about foresight. You will apply it. Because closing the Decision Gap is the way to decide and act differently from the position of stable trajectory, while there is still time.

This is a journey in which you will have to actively participate. It's time to start closing the Decision Gap by playing in the futures, taking decisions and testing outcomes.

Where to Go Next

If you have a particular business question that you need to answer, feel free to jump straight to Part II and whichever of the five Strategic Futures Labs feels most relevant and valuable at this time. You can always return to the other chapters in Part I between completing the exercises set out in the Labs.

But if you'd like to better understand where organizational approaches to strategy developed from, dive into Chapter 2.

2 Past, Present and Future of Strategy

Why traditional strategy collapses under uncertainty. The evolution of strategy from military origins to the Living Company and the mindset shift required for futures work.

All's fair in love and war, or so the saying goes.

However, in business, strategies based solely on competition and conflict are becoming increasingly obsolete and must evolve significantly.

Listen closely to the language of business, and you'll often hear echoes of warfare. Markets become battlegrounds, competitors are framed as adversaries and success is measured by the ground we gain — the market share we capture. Our strategies revolve around threats and targets. Triumph is defined by outmanoeuvring the 'enemy', aka the competition.

This combative mindset has guided the corporate playbooks for decades, but the world has changed and is continuing to do so. It's faster, messier and a lot more interconnected and complex. That means this war-like approach is not just outdated, it's dangerous. To understand why, let's explore this recent cautionary tale.

Peloton: When Military Strategy Meets the Contemporary Market Reality

Peloton is a brand that skyrocketed in sales during the COVID-19 pandemic. The spectacular rise and fall of the brand value is a perfect and modern example of why military-style strategic thinking isn't the best way forward when you operate in an interconnected business world. In January 2021, Peloton's stock peaked at $171.09 per share, with the company reaching a market valuation of close to $50 billion.[1] Can you guess what the stock cost in July 2022, just 18 months later? It dropped by more than 95%, crashing to approximately $8 per share.[2] What a dramatic fall.

The company's strategy was an aggressive military operation that was quite short-sighted in nature. They chose to vertically integrate to control every single aspect of the at-home fitness experience.[3] They were seeking to dominate the battlefield and they mistook an obvious temporary trend for a permanent shift. They over-invested in infrastructure. They spent and hired excessively. They grabbed as much share as they could. But they did not plan for a post-pandemic reality, and they didn't think about the needs of people in the future. The problem wasn't only the shifting market conditions, but also the unwillingness to adapt the approach to fit these emerging needs. Instead, they maintained a fortress mentality, treating every potential partner as a threat, rather than an opportunity to collaborate. This wasn't just a failure of execution. It was the result of a strategic mindset built for control and domination. These are instincts that make sense on a battlefield, but break down in an interconnected market.

In contrast, during the same challenging period for humanity, other brands clearly understood that this type of rigid control in an interconnected world could quickly lead to irrelevance. One example is Fitness+ by Apple, which launched as a software service working across multiple device types and now holds approximately 17% market share in the fitness app market.[4] Strava didn't force users into proprietary hardware; it connected to every device and app and became the dominant fitness social network for amateurs and athletes by blending metrics and social media features. Interestingly enough, Strava began a formal collaboration with Apple Fitness+ on 3 January 2025, allowing Fitness+ workouts to be posted to Strava with rich, redesigned summaries. It seems this collaborative strategy was more long-term based, more additive versus extractive and took into account the transient nature of the trend in 2020.

If you really think about it, it is obvious that people who were stuck at home for long periods of time with no access to nature and the outdoors, would want to experience more of that once they were no longer forced into lockdown. Of course, there were many unknowns and in the face of such dramatic change and uncertainty, we can't know the outcomes. But equally, why do we assume that planning in the standard linear way is right? With this hindsight, it's easy to say that a renewed love for the outdoors among its customers is one possible scenario Peloton should have planned for. But they failed in planning for the post-pandemic world. They failed in practicing foresight — the disciplined ability to envision and prepare for multiple possible futures.

Peloton also illustrates a deeper strategic issue: a single assumed future was embedded into hiring decisions, supply chain commitments, cost structures and therefore investor expectations. Once capital is deployed around one trajectory, flexibility collapses. This is how linear strategy fails in non-linear environments because commitments are structured around continuity rather than conditionality, even though a lot of times the data that can indicate conditionality is available.

This aggressive, win-at-all-costs mentality that shaped Peloton's trajectory is not a new phenomenon. It's inherited through decades and even centuries and has formed part of the corporate DNA. The time has come to question its relevance to the world around us. But to understand the future of strategy better, we must go back — way back.

The Origins of Strategy

We go back not for pure nostalgia, but because strategy is shaped by instinct as much as it is shaped by theory. The early intellectual foundations of strategy were born in environments of conflict, control, secrecy and zero-sum competition. Those instincts to dominate, defend, predict and outmaneuver still quietly influence how many corporations plan today. When conditions are stable, these instincts can drive efficiency. When environments become interconnected and discontinuous, the same instincts can narrow perception and create fragility.

When we think about business strategy, one of the first names that comes to mind is Boston Consulting Group (BCG). Modern business strategy consulting can be traced back to the inception of BCG in 1963. The group began as a branch of The Boston Safe Deposit and Trust Company, initially with just one employee — Bruce Henderson. As the company developed its vision, they searched for which aspects of consulting they could specialize in. It needed to be something bold, and something that other companies hadn't already marked out as their own territory. Henderson focused on the term 'business strategy consultants' to help define the niche itself. In this way, and this was his argument against those in the company who said it was too vague, BCG could shape the definition of strategy itself, rather than be constrained by existing interpretations.

BCG broke ground in business strategy. Previously, the concepts of 'strategy', 'intelligence', and 'foresight' had primarily been associated with the military.

Military strategy hadn't been systematically applied to business before. Until BCG proposed a new approach, it was common to take advice from the original strategists — military thinkers — and use it to guide business decisions.

To help explain why in strategy today we often default to language rooted in military doctrine that signals confrontation, market domination, targets or defeating an opponent, we need to trace it back to its origins. This brings us to one of the earliest recorded moments when strategy became an intellectual discipline, not just a battlefield instinct. Long before boardrooms and consultants, strategy was shaped in entirely different arenas: on battlefields and in empires.

The Warring States period of Chinese history was characterized by constant and perpetual fighting between the seven states. The ongoing wars from 475 BCE to 221 BCE saw constant bloodshed with each state trying to outmanoeuvre the others. They weren't just developing tactics. They were laying the foundations of strategic thinking. And this marked the origins of the first 'strategy consultants' — traveling philosophers for hire, who made their living by giving advice on how to conduct war. One of the most notable of these was Sun Tzu, the often attributed author of *The Art of War*.[5] This concise volume has lasted through the centuries and found a place with many entrepreneurs, sports coaches and others looking for strategy inspiration.

Through *The Art of War*, Sun Tzu describes the use of spies, deceptions and preparation as strategies to ensure victory, often by avoiding conflict altogether. His argument is that the war is so often won away from the battlefield. It's not hard to see why these ideas resonate in both sports and business, where foresight and adaptability are vital. Some notable quotes include:

'Victorious warriors win first and then go to war, while defeated warriors go to war first and then seek to win'.

'If you know the enemy and know yourself, you need not fear the result of a hundred battles'.

These concepts make an effective strategy when you're competing or when it's a zero-sum game — it's win or lose; success or defeat. When only one side can win, like in war or sports, these nuggets of wisdom can be powerful.

In theory, therefore, these principles are not wrong. The problem is that modern business rarely operates as a contained, zero-sum battlefield. Companies do not exist in isolation. They operate inside ecosystems shaped by regulators, suppliers, technology platforms, geopolitical forces and societal expectations. In such systems, success is not solely determined by defeating a rival. It is shaped by adaptation to evolving conditions that no single player controls.

Today we can understand that approaching a battlefield with a strategy is far more effective than simply running our soldiers into their soldiers and seeing who comes out on top. It is common practice for a sports team to have scouting reports on the rival teams, to know what plays they call, the strengths and weaknesses of the players and the team, and to plan appropriately. Understanding the strategies of chess helps players act accordingly and return with their own strategy to nullify the approach of the other player. This zero-sum thinking is simply outdated in business today and is becoming even less relevant in the businesses of the future.

Taking the view that business is adversarial these days is simply short-sighted. There will most likely be competitors to you, but building a company's mindset strictly on defeating the chosen enemy leaves the company at a disadvantage on many other 'fronts', to use another military term. Being the first in terms of market share as a sole objective is no longer enough or relevant. The expectations of companies from their stakeholders go far beyond that. The reason for this lies in the shifting societal values, macro dynamics and humanity facing wicked problems — problems that don't have just one simple solution, which demand all hands on deck.

Today's business is a dynamic, living system, while the military-inspired strategy aims to dominate a field that is static.

If military strategy is not the way to go, then how should we be approaching strategy in business?

Defining a Future-ready Strategy

A future-ready strategy reframes what planning is meant to achieve. Instead of defending a single projected path, strategy becomes a portfolio of conditioned commitments. These are investments designed to remain viable across multiple plausible environments. This requires three disciplined moves:

1. **Expand the view** beyond industry *competitors* to include regulatory, technological, societal and infrastructure forces shaping the rules of the game.
2. **Test commitments against alternative conditions** before capital is locked in, identifying where exposure could be concentrating too much.
3. **Structure investments with checkpoints** that allow acceleration, redesign or exit as signals evolve.

This approach strengthens decisiveness by aligning commitment with awareness of structural change.

The failure to imagine alternative futures and only focus on the short-term is at the heart of what we are going to explore next.

The Innovator's Dilemma: A Turning Point

Companies operating like an army isn't the only problem. Another trap they fall into is the lure of their own success.

Companies are generally great at practicing short-term thinking. They find something that brings them success and tend to just do more of what works today, failing to understand that what works today might be the exact thing that kills them tomorrow. Even those that claim to be innovative rarely embrace the high risk of failure that comes with radical innovation. Instead, they just iterate and take small and cautious steps into the future, mistaking movement for momentum. Why? Because the systems that reward today's success don't take into account tomorrow's threats.

Harvard professor Clayton Christensen famously called it 'The Innovator's Dilemma'.[6] This is the idea that the systems and practices that make a company successful can be the very systems that may ensure its downfall.

At the heart of the dilemma is the tension: companies listen to customers today. They are built to serve their current customers, deliver profits and improve products they already sell. By doing so, they ignore and underinvest in innovations that could secure future success and future customer needs. They take this approach because these innovations are risky and they partially have to disrupt their current model that works so well! They become very smart in repetition and slight iteration — and it works, in the short term. Until that same innovation they could have owned comes along and disrupts their business model. And this disruption comes not because they were not smart enough. They were smart, but in a completely different game. Their strategy has made them rigid and insensitive to external threats and opportunities, because it assumes a stable environment, when the outside world rarely is one.

Christensen's insight is not only about disruption and failure, it's about the structural blindness that repeatedly ignores what doesn't fit in your success model today.

For senior leaders, the incentive system, performance metrics and financial flows are optimized around the current business models. It's this fact that makes this consequential. That type of optimization can unintentionally suppress experimentation in adjacent or emerging spaces. Over time, the organization becomes exceptionally efficient at refining yesterday's advantage, while weakening its ability to position for tomorrow's discontinuity.

So the question Christensen asks is: are you willing to disrupt yourself before someone else does it for you?

There are many well-known examples of companies falling into the Innovator's Dilemma — Blockbuster dismissing Netflix's mail-order service proposal, which cost them their business; Kodak's inventing the digital camera, yet missing the opportunity to lead the digital revolution and filing for bankruptcy in 2012; BlackBerry, once the undisputed mobile communications leader, dismissing the touchscreen smartphone.

Another example is Sony, the proud creator of the Walkman, ultimately losing the on-the-go music market to the iPod. Sony tried to protect their existing CD and MiniDisc business, instead of foreseeing the serious impact of MP3 technology.

What if the real challenge is not choosing between short-term success and planning for a successful tomorrow? What if it is about learning how to balance the two?

Ambidexterity in Business

In mythology there is the legend of Janus, a Roman god of beginnings and endings, doorways, gates and time. Janus has two faces, one looking at the past and the other looking at the future. Janus is one of the most ancient gods and he's often invoked when we talk about ambidexterity and foresight, because he has been gifted the ability to see both into the past and into the future.

Ambidextrous (adj.):

Able to use the right and left hands equally well.

(figurative) Able to use or function in more than one way; versatile or adaptable in action or thought.

Tushman and O'Reilly suggested that in order to ensure long-term survival, a company has to have '… the ability to simultaneously pursue both incremental and discontinuous innovation … from hosting multiple contradictory structures, processes, and cultures within the same firm'.[7]

They introduced the concept of ambidexterity and 'exploit' and 'explore', arguing that a company has a specific organization, skill set and tools to exploit existing resources and opportunities 'to compete in mature technologies and markets where efficiency, control and incremental improvement are prized and to also compete in new technologies and markets where flexibility, autonomy and experimentation are needed'.[8]

In their research, Tushman and O'Reilly observed that companies operating in less volatile external environments had a structured organizational hierarchy, clearly defined roles and responsibilities, categorizing them as 'mechanistic management systems'. By nature, these companies were focused on efficiency, reducing uncertainty and variables, control and were biased towards short-term success. While firms operating in more turbulent environments had more 'organic' systems with less formalized and hierarchical structures, less reliance on specialization and more focus on exploration, innovation, discovery and autonomy. In order for a company to be successful, the two approaches should be well balanced.

The difficulty in achieving this balance is that there is a bias in favour of exploitation with its greater certainty of short-term success. Exploration, by its nature, is inefficient and is associated with an unavoidable increase in the number of bad ideas. Yet, without some effort toward exploration, firms are likely to fail in the face of change.

Let's take a practical view here. Ambidexterity is not about inspirational slogans that support innovation. It is supposed to be about structural separation and leadership discipline. Mature organizations that successfully balance exploitation and exploration often protect these exploratory resource and capital investments with specific governance processes, longer evaluation horizons and different KPIs. Without that deliberate structural protection, exploration is repeatedly deprioritized when short-term pressures intensify. That also impacts morale.

One of the most important learnings is that various studies confirm that there is a positive correlation between the level of ambidexterity and organizational success, measured by sales growth, subjective ratings of performance, market valuation, innovation and firm survival.

René Rohrbeck and his colleagues go further. They have created a quantifiable scoring system to evaluate the Future Preparedness (FP) of a firm by measuring the need for Corporate Foresight (CF), which is an excellent tool for 'exploration' and then comparing it to the sophistication of the CF practices within the firm. Rohrbeck based the results on a survey of 77 large companies and concluded that:

Formal 'strategic foresight' efforts add value through (1) an enhanced capacity to perceive change, (2) an enhanced capacity to interpret and respond to change, (3) influence on other actors, and (4) an enhanced capacity for organizational learning.[9]

Ambidexterity addresses how organizations balance efficiency and exploration. The concept we'll explore next, the Living Company, extends that thinking a step further — from balancing activities to redefining what a company is. Arie de Geus proposed that organizations should not be viewed simply as economic machines designed for shareholder profits, but as living systems capable of learning, adapting and living across generations.

The Living Company

In the early 1980s, as Royal Dutch Shell was starting to think about the company approaching its centenary, the team decided to look at other companies that were older, to attempt to decode the success through the ages. The average lifespan of a company today is less than 20 years. At one end there are those that struggle to make it out of the start-up and incubation phase. At the far end of the spectrum, there are those around the globe that last for hundreds of years. Such examples include companies like Sweden's Stora Kopparberg, the oldest joint stock company in the world, with the first preserved share document from 1288, or Japan's Kongo Gumi, founded in 578 CE, when a temple carpenter from Korea was commissioned by Prince Shōtoku to build the Shitennōji temple in Osaka. It operated continuously for over 1,400 years as an independent family business until being acquired and becoming a subsidiary of Takamatsu Construction Group in January 2006.

When looking for the longest-lasting companies de Geus, who was part of the Shell scenarios team in the 1980s, found about 30 that were older than Shell and that had a recorded history.

His team looked for the common characteristics between these companies that could explain their success and longevity. They found four clear traits that span across all of these companies.

De Geus speaks of their traits:

'… have personality that allows them to evolve harmoniously'.

They know who they are, understand how they fit into the world, value new ideas and new people, and manage their money wisely, in a way that allows them to govern their future.

Those personality traits manifest themselves in behaviours designed to renew the company over many generations.

Throughout, living companies produce goods and services to earn their keep in the same way that most of us have jobs in order to live our lives'.[10]

Here are the key characteristics of these companies as described by de Geus:

1. **'They were conservative in financing'.**
   These companies understood the power of resources and the independence and advantage it can give to a company. They didn't spend recklessly, unlike our earlier Peloton example.
2. **'They had sensitivity to the world around them and were good at "change management"'.**
   The living companies had a great sense of what was happening in the surrounding environment, were able to adapt to it in a timely manner and capture opportunities or escape threats. They were good at learning and re-learning.
3. **'They had a clear awareness of their identity'.**
   The successful companies diversified, but no matter how vast the range of businesses was, every employee felt like part of a whole.

It is important to know what your company stands for, or to put it another way, to know 'what is the theory of your firm'.[11] In other words, it's essential for the employees to feel a sense of belonging. This also applies to organizations that contain many subsidiaries. For example, Lord Cole, chairman of Unilever in the 1960s ... saw the company as a fleet of ships. Each ship was independent, but the whole fleet was greater than the sum of its parts.

4. **'They had high tolerance for new ideas'.**
   All companies in the study proved to have tolerated experiments and eccentricities, recognizing the future may bring an opportunity for a new business that is unrelated to the current business.

Not coincidentally, the last three traits are also traits of strategic foresight!

While some of the companies de Geus studied held onto specific industries or products, like many European breweries or Asian construction companies, others changed their operations with the times. These companies stood by their core principles and understood what the company was good at, but were also open to new ideas. Stora, for example, has roots as a copper mining and forestry company. Today it is more focused on paper products. There were other characteristics that de Geus noted linked with philosophy to financial management, but one key shared trait was the ability of the company to adapt — not overextend.

The Finnish company, Nokia, was able to adapt to take advantage of the tech boom in the early 2000s to become the mobile phone giant it's known as today. Its roots lie in paper pulp, forestry and rubber manufacturing. Nintendo similarly adapted their position after starting as a playing card manufacturer in the late 1800s.

Interestingly, the BCG's Bruce Henderson also observed in his post-retirement writings that there is a strong link between biology and the success of a company. Where commercial or capitalistic competition is often aimed at the previously mentioned win-lose axis and defeating the others, biological success doesn't necessarily mean completely defeating the rival.

A company doesn't exist in isolation or in a made-up reality only within its own industry. It exists in a complex ecosystem and is influenced by and influences all other elements in this ecosystem. Considering factors outside the company but within the environment is therefore essential to gain a deeper understanding of the world as it is today, how it may change in the future, how this will influence the needs and wants of the stakeholders and therefore, the future choices and strategies of the company.

This is where military metaphors begin to unravel. In war, you choose your battlefield. You concentrate your resources. In ecosystems, you don't fight a single battle. You move with the climate, with the others around you. You adapt. Ambidexterity, at its heart, is a living system's survival instinct.

In ecosystems, we don't look for dominance to survive, we look for adaptability. The companies that are great at navigating complexity are those with the most flexible minds and dual capabilities — they can focus on what works today, while prototyping what may work tomorrow. That's at the heart of what it means to become a Living Company through ambidexterity. It's the living system's survival instinct. And it's also where strategic foresight begins — a disciplined capacity to imagine and prepare for what may come tomorrow.

From Shareholder Primacy to Mutuality

As organizations grow in scale and influence, the question of what they exist for becomes impossible to ignore.

Many global corporations today have market capitalizations that rival or exceed the annual economic output of entire countries. While market capitalization and GDP measure different things, the comparison is still revealing: it highlights the scale of influence large corporations wield over employment, innovation, supply chains, culture and environmental outcomes. With that influence comes responsibility — whether organizations explicitly choose it or not.

This tension sits at the heart of what has come to be known as the Economics of Mutuality.[12]

Developed through collaboration between academics, business leaders and practitioners — and strongly associated with work emerging from Mars Inc., and scholars such as Colin Mayer — the Economics of Mutuality challenges the idea that the primary purpose of a firm is short-term shareholder value alone.

Instead, it proposes a simple but profound shift.

In volatile systems, legitimacy affects performance. Talent attraction, capital access, customer loyalty — they all increasingly depend on how the organization shows up in the ecosystem and interacts with it. Mutuality is not a reputational extra benefit, it's in fact a strategic predisposition (or condition) for long-term growth and resilience.

Therefore, long-term economic success depends on creating mutual value for all stakeholders the organization relies on — not extracting value from them.

This includes customers, employees, suppliers, communities, ecosystems and future generations — not as a moral add-on, but as a strategic necessity.

Why This Matters for the Organization of the Future

In a stable world, extractive models can persist for a long time before consequences become visible. In a complex, interconnected world, those consequences surface faster — and often in unexpected ways.

Supply chains break. Talent disengages. Trust erodes. Regulation tightens. Brand value collapses. Systems push back.

The Economics of Mutuality aligns closely with the idea of the Living Company: organizations that endure are those that understand themselves as embedded in ecosystems, not positioned above them.

From a futures perspective, this matters because:

- Value creation is increasingly systemic, not isolated.
- Risk is increasingly shared, not contained.
- Legitimacy becomes a strategic asset.
- Resilience depends on the health of the system around you.

This is not about abandoning profit, but about recognizing that profit is an outcome of a healthy system, not its sole purpose.

A future-ready organization needs a different internal architecture.

Taken together, the Living Company, the Economics of Mutuality and futures thinking, point to a common conclusion:

The organization of the future must be designed differently, not just structurally, but cognitively and strategically.

To translate this shift into practice, I use a simple organizing lens: the ACT Framework. This stands for: Adaptive systems, Conditional strategy, Transformative practice.

Adaptive Systems Organizations must be able to sense change, learn quickly and reconfigure without waiting for the once-a-year opportunity to input into the annual planning cycles. This includes information flows, governance, incentives and decision rights that can adapt as conditions evolve.

Conditional Strategy Strategy must move beyond a single linear plan. It becomes a portfolio of choices, designed to remain resilient and viable across different future realities. Conditional strategy balances performance today with options that preserve relevance tomorrow, recognizing that value creation depends on the health of the broader ecosystem in which the organization operates and not just the internal efficiency.

Transformative Practice In complex environments, incremental improvement is not always enough. Organizations need the capacity to experiment, partner and — at times — redefine how they create value for society and the system they depend on. Mutuality becomes strategic when transformation is intentional.

The ACT framework does not replace strategy. It reframes what strategy is for — not prediction and dominance, but long-term sustained relevance in a world full of uncertainty.

And it sets the foundation for the Strategic Futures Labs that follow, which are designed to build exactly these capabilities, one decision at a time.

Where To Go Next

Now that you better understand the origins of strategy, you may feel you are ready for the Strategic Futures Labs. Feel free to skip ahead if you can now see which of the five questions posed by these Labs would be most valuable for you and your organization at this point.

Hopefully these initial chapters have provided you with language and research to encourage others in your organization to embrace foresight as part of your organization's strategic planning.

In Chapter 3, we'll examine where the Decision Gap lives — and how you can begin to build systems to not only uncover it, but bridge it.

3 Decision-making in Times of Uncertainty

Systems thinking, cognitive bias, behavioural strategy and futures intelligence. Preparing the mind for working across multiple futures.

Chapter 1 defined the Decision Gap. Chapter 2 explained why traditional strategy models often reinforce the Gap. This chapter goes deeper into how decisions are actually made under uncertainty. Because even when leaders see the signals and accept the need for change intellectually, they often struggle to take action. This isn't their fault. It's because, structurally, the system, cognitive biases and incentives often pull them back toward continuity. If foresight is to influence action, the decision-making process and practice itself must be redesigned.

Complexity Is Not Complicated

Here's why linear thinking fails.

Businesses often perceive uncertainty as an information problem. If we can only collect more data, commission better research, create more detailed spreadsheets and more sophisticated models, the right answer will jump at us from the page. This approach makes sense in a world where cause and effect correlate predictably. But in many strategic decisions, the problem is not lack of information. It is actually being overwhelmed by too much information that is the issue. The environment hasn't just become more uncertain, it now works differently. Cause and effect are no longer directly related, so more data doesn't lead to clearer decisions.

Complicated problems can be analysed to find solutions. But complex problems require us to understand their dynamics.

It helps to start with a simple distinction:

Complicated challenges can be difficult and multi-layered, but cause and effect can be identified through expert analysis. The right answer can be found with enough skill and data, even if the problems are intricate.

Complex challenges consist of interdependencies, emergence, feedback loops, adaptation and the outcomes emerge from these dynamically interacting factors. They can only be understood in hindsight. Intervening with the system changes it, and cause and effect cannot be reliably predicted in advance.

This distinction is central to the Cynefin framework.[1] It's a framework widely used in leadership and decision-making context as it offers a practical way to distinguish between 'ordered contexts', where cause and effect are discoverable or clear, and 'unordered contexts', where they are not. In unordered contexts this means leaders must probe–sense–respond rather than assume the right answer will be derived through analysis alone.

We are not talking about semantics here. If you misdiagnose the context, you will apply the wrong logic. The logic that fails under complexity is often some version of linear thinking.

Non-linearity: Why 'More Effort' Doesn't Reliably Create 'More Outcome'

The inputs and outputs of linear systems are usually proportional. If you increase the fuel by 15%, you will increase the range roughly by 15% too, which means that you can measure all of the variables and forecast the trajectory.

Complex systems don't behave the same way.

One reason is the non-linearity — cause and effect don't move in a straight line, they travel through networks of multiple interactions and often these interactions generate feedback. In a system with feedback present, one small change can have a major impact because it can generate a large effect. On the other hand, a large intervention can produce very little change, because the system absorbs it.[2]

This is why 'better answers' can be the wrong goal to chase after. The problem is not the lack of intelligence, as I've explained. The problem is that under complexity, the environment can't be treated as a stable backdrop for decision-making.

The End of Isolated Disruption

Today, change rarely happens as a single, contained event and that's the second reason linear strategy is not the most resilient option for the future.

Companies often prepare for the disruptions one at a time — one tech shift, one crisis, one competitor innovation, one regulatory change. But what actually happens in real life is based on interaction. Disruptions overlap, reshape one another and compound to create a high impact that we are not usually prepared for.

In healthcare, for example, a hospital system may plan for aging demographics as a steady increase in demand, yet face simultaneous workforce shortages, digital health adoption, funding reform and regulatory changes. The impact does not come from a single trend, but from the interaction among them.

In the technology industry, companies may optimize engagement metrics, while underestimating regulatory momentum and public trust dynamics. By the time governance changes reshape the operating environment, strategic positioning has already been put in place and focused on assumptions that are no longer true.

Systemic shocks are described by Roger Spitz as 'metaruptions'. He uses this term to describe 'multidimensional' and 'systemic' disruptions, not just single events, but their interaction that sometimes redefines what disruption even means.[3]

Whether you adopt the term or not is not important. What matters is that extrapolating a single trend into the future and basing decisions on this prediction when disruptions interact is not a solid plan. You are operating in a field of interrelated forces and have to gain the skills and acquire the tools to navigate it.

Problems Behave Differently Now

The issue is not a matter of intelligence. It is a matter of asking the right questions, working with the right tools, and adopting a new mindset — you must think differently.

Complicated contexts require a future path that follows the principle: analyse, optimize, execute.

This approach, however, can cause false confidence in complex contexts, because through analysis you're trying to extract certainty from a system that simply won't give it!

That is the reason a future-ready strategy starts upstream of tools like scenarios and future narratives.

It starts with a diagnostic realization:

Not all problems are created equal. Not everything can be solved by more precision. Some challenges require different logic altogether.

This is the first step towards future readiness — realizing that you're no longer in a world where linear planning works reliably.

The Human System Inside the Organization

If complexity theory explains why linear strategy fails, then human cognition explains why insight alone does not change behaviour (or invoke action). It also explains why good information doesn't necessarily lead to good decisions.

A consistent pattern, almost universally, is observed across companies: teams generate high-quality research, deliver great analytical reasoning and then highlight a credible threat. They even acknowledge uncertainty, but, following all that, they proceed with decisions that are almost identical to those they would have made without that intelligence.

This isn't caused by lack of experience, it's simply how human decision-making works under uncertainty.

We don't act on data — we act on meaning.

Decades of behavioural decision-making and cognitive psychology research show that people don't interpret information objectively and neutrally. As humans, we construct meaning through mental models. We create these simplified stories in our minds that help us navigate a complex world with our limited cognitive resources.

A great way to understand this concept is through the ladder of inference, pioneered by Chris Argyris and later made popular in various organizational learning, cultural and foresight contexts.[4,5]

It shows how people move rapidly from observable data to selected data, to interpretations, assumptions and finally conclusions that feel like 'facts'. And once these conclusions are reached, they feed back into what data is monitored, noticed and selected next time, reinforcing the story. What Argyris explains is that the journey through the ladder of inference (Figure 3.1) is different for each one of us. It is clouded by subjectivity, induced and reinforced by our cultural environment, upbringing, family influence, experience etc. Our brain always looks for shortcuts and predictions and we can easily fall into the trap of this reflexive loop where our inherent beliefs influence what we observe.

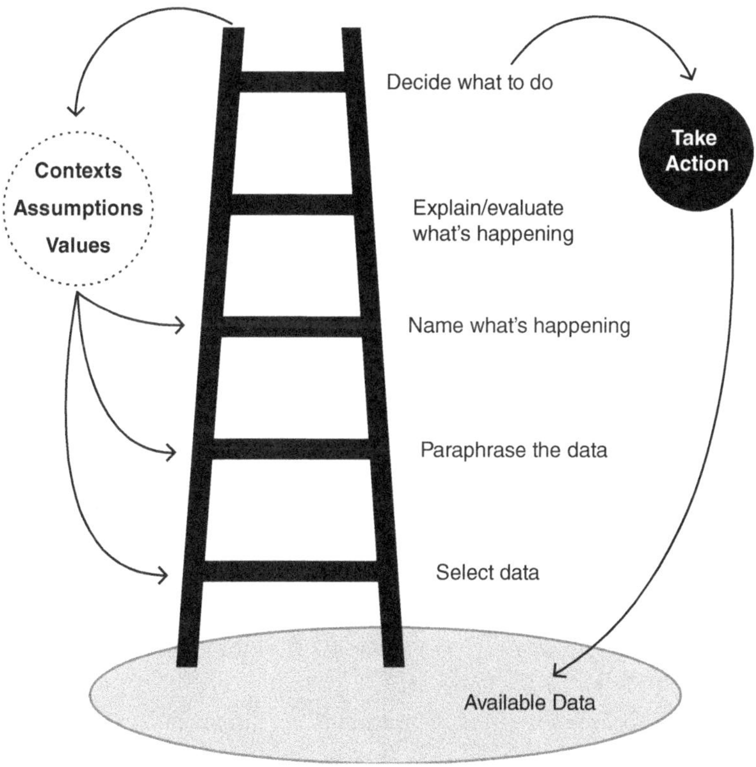

Figure 3.1 The Ladder of Inference.

In a business environment this process happens collectively. Our strategies are stories that illustrate who we are, what we do well and why our achievements are meaningful. Newly presented information that fits the existing narrative is easily absorbed. Information that contradicts it is rejected, delayed or reframed in some way.

I am sure a lot of the insights professionals reading this will recognize themselves in this paragraph. How many presentations have been altered to minimize the uncomfortable truth so that it does not cause disturbance and controversy during a meeting?

This is one of the main reasons foresight is often seen as 'interesting and inspirational', but not 'actionable'. It disrupts established narratives, and when a story no longer fits how an organization understands itself, it is resisted rather than acted upon.

Cognitive Bias Is Not a Bug — It's the Operating System

A large and influential part of the applied bias literature is presented as a checklist of common decision 'errors' to avoid. To me this framing is misleading. Cognitive biases are not flaws we happen to layer on top of rational thinking. They are necessary. After all, this is how we, humans, decide quickly under uncertainty.[6]

Some biases become particularly influential in strategic contexts:

- **Status quo bias:** the preference for the existing situation and arrangements, especially when the alternative is uncertain.[7]
- **Confirmation bias:** the tendency to seek, interpret and action information that supports existing beliefs, while discounting evidence that disproves them.[8]
- **Loss aversion:** losses seem larger than gains, making the potential downside more psychologically salient than equivalent upside.[9]
- **Success bias:** past and current success increases the confidence that current assumptions will continue to hold, even in a situation where the conditions that caused the success are no longer present.[10]
- **Sunk cost fallacy:** the tendency to continue on the same course of action, because of prior investments — financial, reputational, political — rather than because it remains the best option for the future.[11]

As one rises through the ranks, biases become more entrenched rather than less so, because the stakes amplify the consequences of bias. It is very difficult to challenge strategies in place since they are deeply linked to an established reputation, political alignment and prior commitments.

Where the Decision Gap Lives

The Decision Gap isn't the space between lack of insight and intelligence. It is the gap between awareness and action, between recognition and commitment, between knowing what to do and actually doing it.

When the conditions are changing we should be acting as they have. When there is intellectual agreement, it should lead to a behavioural follow-through. There is a significant difference between the views people express in workshop discussions and the recommendations that are officially accepted in governance forums.

Information alone is not able to close this gap, because the gap is continuously maintained by incentives that reward short-term performance, systems designed for stability, identities built around past success and cognitive shortcuts that favour business continuity over exploration.

Understanding this is absolutely critical. If we treat decision failure as an information issue, we will just keep producing better reports. But if we treat it as a human system problem, we begin to view and design decisions differently.

Let's think about a large technology firm that notices early signals that generative AI could significantly compress margins in its core service model within five years.

A usual response might be focusing on improving forecasts, refining pricing and extracting short-term efficiency gains.

But if you are looking to bridge the Decision Gap, you will need a different sequence:

1. **Surface multiple plausible scenarios.** What if adoption accelerates quickly? What if regulatory changes slow implementation? What if the customers' expectations are that automation is in fact a baseline feature?
2. **Stress-test the current revenue model against these variations.** Under which conditions does the model become structurally vulnerable?
3. **Design conditional commitments.** Make small but meaningful investments that preserve strategic options rather than locking in exposure.
4. **Establish governance checkpoints** tied to leading indicators rather than lagging financial outcomes. This is a really important step.

None of these steps will require certainty, they just require earlier commitment under uncertainty, but that is precisely where most organizations hesitate.

Systems Thinking

How to See the Structure Beneath Events If business decisions are shaped by the human systems and are linked with the systems in which they take place, then strategy has to be informed by systems thinking. This means the ability to see patterns where others see noise, and to recognize relationships and structures rather than see the isolated events in a system.

From Events to Structures Donella Meadows describes systems as 'an interconnected set of elements that is coherently organized in a way that achieves something'.[12] Real understanding of a system's behaviour is not based on how it is seen at any one time, but it is about why it keeps happening. The Iceberg Model (Figure 3.2) from systems thinking, popularized by Senge,[13] illustrates how visible events are shaped by deeper patterns, system structures and mental models.

The Iceberg Model is widely used:

- At the surface are events: what has just occurred.
- Below are patterns and trends: what has been happening over time.
- Deeper still are structures: rules, relationships, flows, incentives.
- At the base are mental models: beliefs and assumptions that shape the system.

Organizational responses largely centre on events. Operating effectively in situations of uncertainty requires leaders to adopt a more adaptive, learning approach that engages with complexity. This is only possible when leaders pay attention to the mental models that they and others use in their thinking. They also need to be aware of the structures which they and their organizations use to handle information and make decisions.

One of the key concepts in foresight is to search for underlying factors driving events rather than merely examining surface appearances. The distinguished futures scholar Professor Sohail Inayatullah has described this layered way of seeing through the Causal Layered Analysis (Figure 3.3).[14]

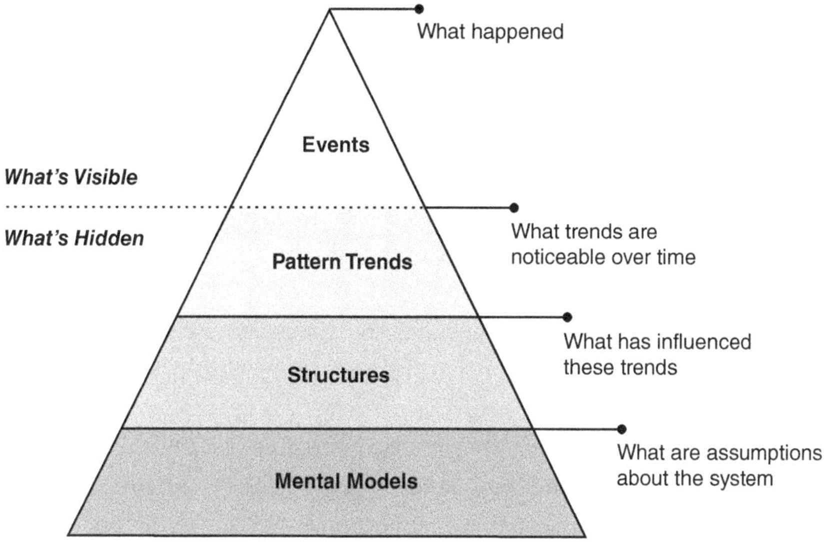

Figure 3.2 The Iceberg Model.

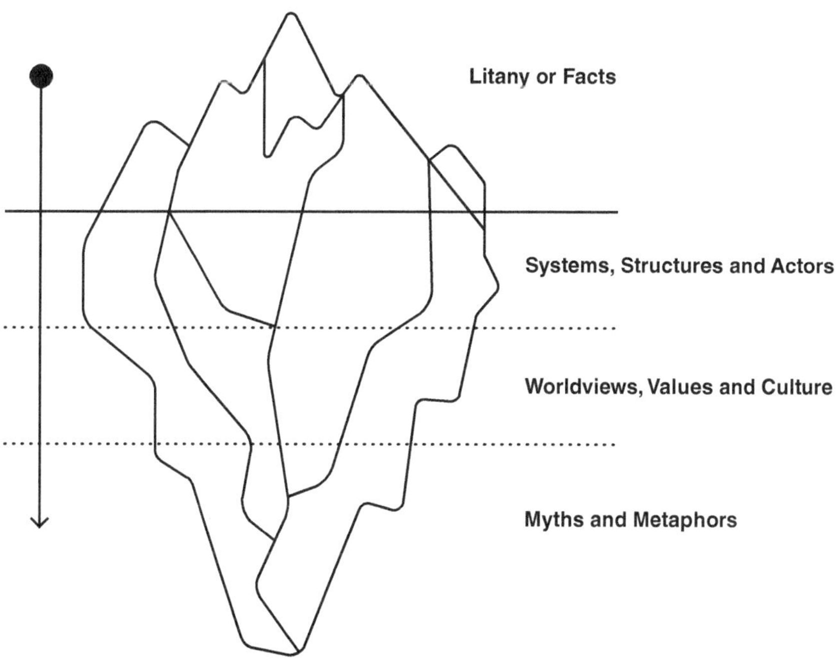

Figure 3.3 Causal Layered Analysis (CLA).

On the surface, leaders debate facts, metrics and trends. Beneath these lie the structures like incentives, governance models and power relationships which mould people's behaviour. Deeper still are shared beliefs about what success looks like, what is considered 'realistic', and what kinds of futures feel legitimate to pursue. At the deepest layer are the metaphors and narratives organizations live by, such as the stories of competition, growth, control or disruption, that quietly define what feels possible or impossible long before a strategy discussions begin.

From a decision-making perspective, this matters because strategies rarely fail at the level of analysis. They fail at the level of these deeper layers. If the underlying story remains unchanged, when new facts become available, they are either reframed to fit with the current knowledge, ignored or else absorbed in ways that do not affect the original theory. By exclusively reacting to what has already occurred or what is happening now, we frequently encounter surprising events or trends that could have been predicted. In order to bring about significant strategic change, leaders need to understand that this kind of change requires working across all levels of the iceberg. That means the structures and plans of the organization, as well as its underlying assumptions and dominant narratives.

Feedback Loops and Unintended Consequences

Actions and interventions in complex systems generate feedback. Some of this feedback reinforces behaviour (reinforcing loops), other feedback restrains behaviour (balancing loops).[15]

For example:

- Improvements in efficiency can yield gains in the short term, which serve to perpetuate a situation where there is exploitation of existing ideas, products and resources. Unfortunately this could be happening at the cost of a gradual erosion of the capability to explore new ideas that might be the only potential profit generator in the future.
- Cutting costs can sometimes leave a company in a vulnerable position if it is hit by a setback.
- The provision of incentives for growth can result in a significant increase in risk taking until constraints are hit abruptly.

One consequence of delayed and dispersed feedback is that the cause and effect are frequently separated by both space and time. The well-intentioned measures I've just outlined therefore often lead to unforeseen repercussions.

Leverage Points: Where Change Actually Works

Scientific research by Donella Meadows reveals that in complex systems not all interventions are created equal.

Essentially, modifying targets, key performance indicators or budget is easy, but usually, this will not have any significant effect.

Organizations that make changes to the processes, the way information moves around and, most importantly, the purpose and attitudes of their systems, experience much greater influence as a result. However, to do this is significantly harder.

The future-ready organizations and Living Companies are those which don't simply decide on the right things, but are also able to change how decisions are made.

It is crucial that the systems thinking exercise does not replace leadership judgement. The process serves to sharpen this judgement by giving a more accurate assessment of where effort is likely to matter and where the best use of one's time and energy is likely to generate results, as well as where it is likely to be absorbed without any effect.

Decision Exercise: Locate Your Own Decision Gap

Take one strategic initiative currently happening in your organization.

Ask yourself and your leadership team:

- What assumptions about the future must hold true for this initiative to succeed?
- What early signals would indicate those assumptions are weakening?
- Where, in your current governance process, would those signals surface?
- Who would have both the authority and the incentive to act on them?

If these questions do not have clear answers, the gap is structural.

Futures Intelligence (Not Simply Foresight, and Definitely Not Forecasting)

How to Think Forward Without Searching for Certainty in Prediction
In complex and volatile environments, it is not wise to regard the future as a destination to predict. It should be considered a learning space.

The Limits of Prediction As I explained in the Introduction, studies on expert forecasting, most notably led by Philip Tetlock, demonstrate that even highly skilled experts with great credentials, struggle to predict outcomes accurately where uncertainty, complexity and rapid feedback exist. Furthermore, accuracy of predictions tends to decline as time horizons extend.[16]

This does not mean the future is completely unknowable. It just means that we are looking at the wrong thing — prediction is the wrong objective.

Futures Literacy and Anticipatory Capacity According to UNESCO, futures literacy is the capability to use the future to understand the present and expand choices. It is not to get the future right, but to reveal assumptions, explore alternatives and strengthen anticipatory learning.[17]

From Trends to Convergences Another common trap is treating trends as independent forces. In reality, strategic impact emerges from the interaction between various different trends. Complex outcomes arise through a convergence of socio-economic, technological, environmental and political forces.

Scenarios take these interactions and turn them into future narratives. These narratives are not valuable because they describe precisely what will happen (they don't), but because they allow leaders and teams to rehearse decisions across different configurations of these forces of change.

Used well as an additional input into the decision-making process, scenario planning can expose hidden assumptions that no longer stand, stretch our mental models and provide a shared language for uncertainty.

If used as speculative storytelling, scenarios can be very inspirational and entertaining, but when leaders are looking for a connection back to real decisions, delivering a sci-fi story without the appropriate tools will make foresight earn its name as ambiguous and maybe even unnecessary.

This is where foresight becomes futures intelligence — and futures intelligence becomes futures capability.

The Mindset Shift

What Kind of Leader Does Complexity Demand? Let's not forget that tools don't operate in a parallel reality. They should express a certain mindset and lead us toward an outcome.

Working effectively with complexity requires a mindset shift across multiple dimensions. Leaders should transition:

- **From expecting prediction to exploration**
  Instead of asking 'What will happen?', they should be asking 'What could happen, and what would that mean for us?'
- **From efficiency to resilience**
  We trade some efficiency for flexibility, buffers and the ability to adapt.
- **From rigid control to adaptation**
  The authority shifts from enforcing plans to enabling learning and adjustment

This isn't an argument for a lack of organization and discipline, but it's crucial that we learn to be disciplined in our learning, not only in the execution of a task.

Introducing the Future Choice Architecture

At the intersection of behavioural science, systems thinking and foresight sits a powerful idea — decisions about the future are shaped by the way choices are structured as part of a system, not just by the information available.

Future-ready decisions can be designed.

Each strategic choice we make, is shaped by:

- **Visible information**
  What signals, data and perspectives are surfaced to decision-makers and what remains invisible. Dashboards, presentations, reports — they all determine what is noticed and what is ignored.
- **Legitimate futures**
  Which range of possible futures are taken seriously and which are dismissed as irrelevant, uncomfortable or unlikely?

- **Trade-offs**
  How are they framed? Are they presented as an either/or dilemmas or as tensions to be managed over time. That is Growth vs Sustainability instead of Growth AND Sustainability.
- **Risks**
  Which risks are made openly named, discussable and debated vs those that are culturally, politically or reputationally taboo?

The Strategic Futures Labs in the chapters that follow are not designed to generate better predictions, but to help us ask better questions, train the capacity to make better choices under uncertainty and challenge our own assumptions to expand our mindset.

Each of these Labs functions as a rehearsal space, where teams can examine the assumptions, surface uncomfortable signals, stress-test strategies, discover new ways of thinking about a problem, and practice the art of committing to a decision and action toward the future.

As we go through the Labs and continue to make sense of the data and assess the situation, we begin to close the Decision Gap. We are doing this not by eliminating uncertainty but by becoming skilled and confident to decide within it!

PART II Your Strategic Futures Labs

This is where we reach the practical element of this book. Each of the five Strategic Futures Labs included here is designed to be run in isolation, as well as to connect with the others. You do not have to complete them in order.

Start anywhere. Pick the question you need to answer today.

Their purpose is to get you to think differently about the future and to begin to see the multiple future scenarios we could inhabit. These are spaces where you can stress-test your current strategy and examine the assumptions that underpin your entire business.

At times what these Labs reveal will be uncomfortable. In fact, I expect you will find much of what you learn through completing these exercises leads to discomfort. I urge you not to turn away and put this book down. Discomfort is where the real breakthroughs lie. Sit with it. Explore it. Embrace it, even.

These next five chapters are designed to be *done* not to be *read*. The insights you gain will be most profound when you work through the exercises with others on your leadership team rather than in isolation. You can find all the templates for the tools featured in these chapters on www.futures-forward.com.

It's time to bring futures intelligence into the heart of your organization. Let's get started.

4

Strategic Futures Lab 1: Who Is My Customer of the Future?

Tool: Future Living Environment Map

What if the needs your customers have tomorrow are not the ones showing up in today's data? This Strategic Futures Lab is built to help you spot the shift, before it's too late to act on it.

Meet Your Future Self — Your POV

You are the Chief Marketing Officer of a company that prides itself on being truly customer-centric. You rely on a strong segmentation model, have a deep understanding of your customers, and regularly run deep-dive sessions to ensure the customer voice is clearly heard.

You have all the data to prove it. Over the years segmentation models have undergone refinements and the company has invested heavily in validating the personas you have developed. Customer satisfaction and NPS (Net Promoter Score) are through the roof, clearly outperforming the category. And yet, over the last year or so, something is starting to feel misaligned.

Brand campaigns still generate results, but don't travel as far. Their impact is shorter-lived and reaches fewer people organically. Attention is fragmented, algorithms limit reach and messages don't cascade like they used to.

New product launches are seemingly successful. They attract initial interest, but enthusiasm for them fades quicker than before. The early adoption no longer reliably turns into sustained usage, loyalty or word-of-mouth.

Brand trust is harder to read and even harder to predict. Sentiment shifts rapidly, varies across contexts and platforms and can change suddenly.

There is a recurring question at leadership meetings that is phrased in different ways, but always means the same:

'Are we still relevant … or just familiar?'

You are so attuned to the business that you start to wonder if what you are seeing are patterns or if you are imagining problems that don't exist. If it's not broken, why fix it, right? Wrong. These are uncomfortable patterns that are emerging. Customers used to love the brand, they now seem to interact with it transactionally. The social media listening reports show stable and high mentions, but the tone seems flatter, the emotional intensity seems to have slowed down.

The dashboards your team is looking at show stable acquisition costs, steady conversion and churn. But there is something the numbers don't show that you feel in your bones: the energy around the brand has shifted.

The language is defensive in leadership meetings, it isn't ambitious anymore. Nobody is asking, 'Where next?' Everyone seems too preoccupied with, 'How do we ringfence what already works?'

You can sense it, yet you can't prove it. The organization is optimizing, but it's doing so for yesterday's version of loyalty.

And while this isn't a decline in sales yet, it is a shift. And that is even harder to address, because it is hiding behind stable numbers!

The insights team has done everything you asked of them. The data is solid, the numbers hold and every standard metric confirms that customers are understood and satisfied. From their point of view, nothing is broken.

Product development teams echo the same confidence. The roadmap is clearly customer-led, grounded in validated insights and expressed needs, and defensible within the company's existing strategic logic.

Yet your CEO remains concerned by the uncertainty and lack of answers. She wants reassurance that today's performance translates into strong performance tomorrow. The concern is not whether the brand is delivering revenue, but whether it still matters, because growth without legitimacy is fragile, and legitimacy without growth will not be able to sustain the business. Missing the beat on this one can have implications that are not just financial but also reputational.

The stakes are high. If you misread this shift, the consequences may not appear immediately, but they can be substantial. They will start showing up in talent, with employees choosing to work for more culturally aligned brands. Or in investors who start to question if long-term support makes sense. Or in regulators who scrutinize the organizations that extract without contributing. It's expensive and time consuming to recover from a place of lost relevance.

The truth is, the organization and the C-suite are structurally rewarded for short-term optimization, not long-term reinvention. This explains the leadership team's focus on optimizing for what works now and not what may come next.

To convince them to act you need evidence and proof. At the same time, you realize that waiting for a definitive proof may *look* like the responsible thing to do, but in practice it guarantees lateness.

Then one day, at a random workshop that nearly got cancelled, a younger colleague braved a comment which stuck in your mind:

'We need to make sure we are designing for a version of our customers that will live in the future.'

There is no crisis yet, no burning platform, and this makes the question more dangerous, not less. It might be the case of the company headed towards a crisis in slow motion and having no answers as to the reasons, nor a plan to act upon. Because if the customer is changing not just what they buy, but why they choose to buy it, what they value and how they relate to brands, then optimizing what already works may be the riskiest move of all.

This Strategic Futures Lab exists for this moment.

It is designed for pre-emptive clarity, not for a crisis response.

It will ask you to temporarily leave the comfort of a world where your team has validated target audiences and approved roadmaps, and to step into the uncertainty of future conditions.

You are not here to challenge your current segmentation model, but to test whether it can still be relevant when it interacts with a different context.

Because if the reality of your future customer shifts even a little, then your strategy may not be resilient.

If you only look for validation in the present, you may be blindsided by a future you never expected to arrive.

As we explored in Chapter 3, disruptions rarely arrive alone. Social pressure, technological mediation, regulatory shifts and cultural redefinitions overlap. The future customer sits at the intersection of these forces. Ignoring that interaction creates strategic blind spots.

Welcome to Strategic Futures Lab 1

This Lab has been created for a very precise tactical moment.

It isn't here for the moment when performance is declining, but for when everything appears to be working on the surface, yet meaningful relevance feels harder to justify.

It is designed to help leaders slow down and answer four questions that are rarely explored together, but that quietly shape almost every strategic decision:

1. How is the world changing in ways that affect people's lives, not just markets or categories?
2. What would it feel like to live and make choices in those future conditions?
3. Which human needs will rise, collide or become non-negotiable as a result?
4. And so what? Where could it plausibly make sense for us as a brand to matter to the customers in this future?

The Lab's intent is not to predict who the future customers might be, but to clarify the conditions that will shape demand. In doing so, decisions can be made with intent rather than inertia.

This Lab is structured to provide the basis for your strategic rehearsal. It is not meant to be perceived as an exercise in research. You are invited to step into a near-term future context, where the stable customer segment of today is being reshaped by culture, technology and legislation, which leads to shifting behaviours and expectations.

You are intentionally placed inside this future and asked to face an uncomfortable decision. The reason being that this decision needs to be taken well before the numbers clearly prove it's necessary. If you wait for the hard evidence, then you've arrived late. The decision is whether to keep defending an existing market you understand very well or whether to reallocate attention (and investment), and if so how much, toward an emerging segment that is smaller today, but indicates that it is growing.

Just like in real-life situations, you will be offered four distinct strategic paths, each bearing consequences that play out over time. There is no 'right' answer and any answer you take will be the right answer for you. The point here is to make the trade-offs visible and ensure your decision is based on the most up-to-date information available. It is to decide with intent, not from a reactive position under pressure.

By the end of this Strategic Futures Lab, you will not only walk away with insight and foresight, but most importantly, you will produce two things that can be carried into your Futures Strategy Canvas:

1. A clear decision about where your organization should earn relevance in the future.

AND

2. A simple categorization of your market positioning. What is the balance you choose strategically? Are you primarily defending your core? Are you hedging across several segments? Are you aggressively reallocating toward the emerging future customer needs?

A Short Detour: Why We Cannot Start with Our Current Customers

Businesses usually start by assessing their existing customer base.

Segmentation models.

Personas.

Customer journeys.

Jobs to Be Done.

They are each limited in their ability to identify the answers to the question this Lab is asking — these tools are all short-sighted.

The Jobs to Be Done (JTBD) framework fundamentally improved how organizations think about value by shifting attention from products to underlying human goals: what people are 'trying to get done' in a given situation.[1,2] People, it seems, 'hire' products to get things done. It is a useful, but time bound method.

This approach relies on three key assumptions that start to break down when there is a significant change in circumstances.

- Stable context — the situation in which the job occurs is broadly known.
- Human decision-makers — people choose, evaluate and act themselves.
- Known constraints — barriers are visible and current.

In future contexts:

- The situation changes.
- Agency could be delegated to systems.
- Barriers to satisfying the needs (as well as potential solutions) might be completely different to the ones that exist today.

The job might not disappear, but it does change shape.

For futures work, the question becomes:

What job will still need to be done and under what conditions?

Do Human Needs Change?

This question has been debated for decades across psychology, economics and futures studies.

A long tradition argues that human needs are stable and universal, even if the ways they are satisfied evolve. This view appears in the work of Abraham Maslow, and is later made more explicit by Manfred Max-Neef, who distinguishes between enduring human needs and historically contingent satisfiers.[3,4]

At the same time, scholars examining digital life, automation, and surveillance argue that technology reshapes how needs are experienced, prioritized and constrained. Sherry Turkle explores how mediation alters autonomy and identity, while Shoshana Zuboff shows how economic systems can structurally change choice and agency.[5,6]

For the purpose of this experiment, we take a pragmatic stance.

We assume core human needs exist today — and that the future reshapes the conditions under which they are met.

What changes is not the need itself, but:

- The context people live in, and therefore the priority of their needs.
- The barriers they face.
- The solutions available.
- The trade-offs they are willing (or forced) to make.

Strategy fails when organizations confuse current satisfaction with enduring need.

From Customers to Humans in Context

Most organizations are excellent at describing customers today by age, income, preferences and behaviours. What they struggle with is imagining the identities of people inside future worlds.

Foresight can help by separating the three layers of reality, a tool inspired by The Three Environments of Foresight by The Futures School[7] see Figure 4.1.

1. **The external environment**. Social, technological, economic, environmental, political forces shaping the world.
2. **The lived environment**. How those forces shape daily life, identity, agency and constraints.
3. **The decision environment**. How choices are actually made by people, systems, platforms, algorithms.

The Future personas in this Lab live at the intersection of all three.

Future personas are not demographic segments. They are structured representations of humans living inside a specific future context. They combine environment, agency, constraint and priority needs. They are not a representation of better demographics, they are contextualized humans.

Why Personas Despite the Criticism Among the primary tools used in strategy and design, the persona is perhaps the most frequently used and most heavily condemned.

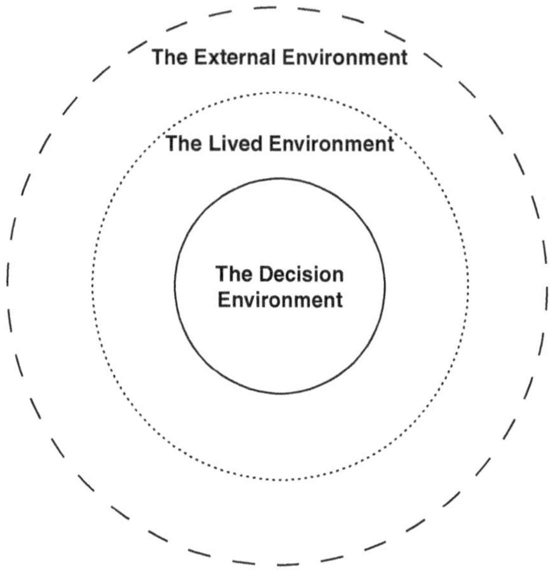

— — **The External Environment**
Social, technological, economic, environmental, political forces shaping the world.

.... **The Lived Environment**
How those forces shape daily life, identity, agency and constraints.

——— **The Decision Environment**
How choices are actually made by people, systems, platforms, algorithms.

Figure 4.1 The Three Layers of Future Reality.

Research has shown that personas can oversimplify reality, reinforce bias and create false confidence when treated as fact rather than hypothesis.[8]

And yet brands don't exist to respond to macro forces, or to punish a competitor, their purpose revolves around actual people and their needs.

'Would someone like this still trust us?'

'What would break for them first?'

'Would our presence still feel legitimate?'

This Lab uses personas deliberately differently. The personas are here to make a human need under pressure inside a specific future context more relatable and discussable.

The Tool: Future Living Environment Map

This Lab combines three established strands of thinking:

- Futures thinking (context and conditions).
- Human needs theory (enduring priorities).
- Jobs to Be Done logic (what people are trying to achieve).

It brings these three strands together into a single, practical tool: the Future Living Environment Map.

You don't have to analyse trends or brainstorm ideas. What you should focus on is prioritizing what must matter to your customers under future conditions.

Step 1 — Start with the Future Worlds

This is where future scenarios come in handy and you will deliberately step into future worlds (see Figure 4.2). You can use scenarios that have been developed internally or commissioned from consultants.

If you don't have your own scenarios, you can head to **www.futures-forward.com** to access a range of resources.

Below are some simplified examples of what these could look like.

These hypothetical situations are not forecasts of future events. They are deliberately constructed pressure contexts designed to stress-test human needs under different structural conditions.

How to Use These Future Scenarios The value of this Lab lies not in finding the 'perfect' future scenario, but in running the exercise and going through the thought process. You will do just fine using these four plausible future contexts, as long as they are meaningfully different from each other and put your customer segments under pressure.

Think of each future as a stress-test for human needs. Each one creates different conditions that squeeze certain needs and elevate others.

Your objective here is not to predict which future will occur. You are exploring how your customers' lives and needs might change if any of these conditions become their everyday reality.

If you choose to, you may attach a degree of plausibility to each future and weight your decision accordingly.

The scenarios that follow are intentionally simple, because the outcome of this Strategic Futures Lab is decision clarity, not narrative sophistication. In addition, you don't always have many data points to make decisions when you operate within an uncertain environment.

In my practice, I often advise clients to go one step further: formulate a clear hypothesis for your segment or organization, based on what you learn from each of the scenarios, and identify the key truths that would need to be in place for that hypothesis to hold. These become the signals your foresight team can monitor for. They're indicators showing whether you are moving towards or away from that anticipated future state.

Short Example: Hypothesis to Signals For example, after exploring the four futures, you might form this simple assumption:

Context: premium athletic footwear brand focusing on 18–25-year-old urban customers.

Hypothesis In the next three to five years, the main focus audience for the brand will be late Gen Z, early Gen Alpha urban customers. They will prioritize verified environmental impact, customizable functional enhancement and culturally authentic design over celebrity endorsements and hype-driven drops when choosing athletic footwear.

This means that beyond the functional benefits, like comfort or performance enhancement, the products would have to allow for customization and co-creation of design with local communities, prioritize authentic and meaningful stories of provenance, and demonstrate sustainability credentials.

All of these will outperform the traditional influencer marketing strategies.

Remember, this is an assumption we are making and we need to ask ourselves, what should be true for this assumption to hold?

These are the signals that should become visible:

- Public critique of 'greenwashing' continues to increase and protests occur against it.
- Regulation becomes tighter around environmental claims and penalties rise.
- Traceability and impact details are actively requested by customers, not just a nice to have.

- Collaborations with niche communities across various industries are praised and make the news when they are done right, and when they aren't.
- Other brands are starting to shift budgets from global ambassadors to localized design partnerships and these are the campaigns that become viral and win awards.

These five items become your monitoring indicators. If these start coming true, then your assumption holds. If the opposite happens, then you need to sense-check your assumption.

How to know you were right: if impact-led, culturally grounded products show that they strengthen brand loyalty and repeat purchases, your hypothesis gains weight.

How to know you were wrong: if hype cycles continue to dominate switching behaviour, you still benefit from this exercise, because you can revisit and adjust your assumption early, not after the relevance of your brand declines.

We are not here to predict, but to observe in a disciplined way and keep our strategy open to adaptation.

Time horizon — choose before you begin: Before you start, choose a horizon that matches your strategic planning cycle. For many leadership teams this is **3–5 years**.

If you are in a highly regulated or asset-heavy industry, you may prefer **5–10 years**.

Future 1: Frictionless but Opaque

What the World Feels Like Everything seems perfectly in order, with life flowing easily. Operations generally run smoothly and delays are unusual.

How Systems Operate Most internet platforms combine a range of services, with default settings designed to suit the average user. It often appears that an endeavour is doing better than it actually is because key indicators are focusing on optimization criteria.

What Daily Life Feels Like It is easy to do this, but few people actually understand what is happening. It is often difficult to know why things have not gone as planned or to know who is accountable when things have gone wrong.

Implications for Customers and Brands This is a future where convenience remains high, but clarity is low.

While it is exciting to be able to benefit from fast speed and to be able to free up cognitive space for other, more pleasant or important tasks, this comes at the expense of growing dependency on systems customers do not fully understand or that they are unable to interrogate. Recommendations are ready-made and already ranked. The outcome is very much driven by the default setting that gets pushed to the customer as the optimal choice.

What a paradox! Life is easier, but agency seems to be slipping away fast. After the novelty wears off, people start to notice that trust comes with conditions. At one point, what everyone starts to care most about is whether the opaque system works in their best interest.

The shift for brands is also evident. They are moving away from emotional storytelling to partnering with the algorithm and ensuring embedded positioning and a higher ranking to ensure visibility. A brand may no longer be chosen by a human, but instead be chosen by an algorithm, acting on someone's behalf. And this brings up questions:

- How do you optimize for system selection?
- How do you explain your value best to a non-human middleman?
- Would you still be chosen if a system evaluated you instead of a person?

In this frictionless but opaque system, brands that don't easily prove their benefit risk being kicked out by the filter before the customer even notices.

Future 2: High Friction, Low Trust

What the World Feels Like Uncertain, tense and volatile. Institutions enjoy a fragile level of public confidence.

How Systems Operate Decisions are still made by people, but the support systems that they have are disorganized and they are not consistent. Openness sets you apart.

What Daily Life Feels Like The burden of making a decision weighs on us. We're all constantly fatigued by the need to make decision after decision without much support or encouragement.

Implications for Customers and Brands This future is defined by system fatigue, while technology and process still very much exist. Everything works somehow. Markets still operate, institutions still exist, but there is fragility in the confidence toward the system.

In this world, customers carry more – emotionally and mentally. Decisions take longer and feel heavier, because the task to evaluate options sits with the individual. There is a lack of trust and a lot more active verification of facts. People have learned that every interaction with a brand, a bank or a media outlet requires heavy scrutiny. Trust is not taken for granted. It has to be repeatedly earned.

Transparency is one of the key differentiators and if you are a brand, especially one that is excessively managed, you will be treated with suspicion by default.

Public sentiment shifts very quickly and the risk of reputational damage is extremely high.

In such a world, each choice requires too much energy. Each purchase requires research and justification. Each subscription requires reconsideration. This context changes how loyalty forms.

In this low-trust environment, loyalty forms by being reliable under pressure, not from visibility and frequency of exposure. Brands are judged less by their promises and more by how they behave in moments of tension. What would they do when pricing shifts, or a product launch fails? How do they behave when there are supply chain disruptions, political bias or cybersecurity attacks?

Brands are being asked very different questions in this context:

- Is there consistency when scrutiny increases and pressure intensifies?
- Are your public commitments and your actions fully aligned?
- If it came to it, would customers take your side?

The only way to grow a brand in this environment is through credibility and dependability.

Future 3: Identity and Belonging First

What the World Feels Like Deep divisions exist between various sections of the society. Public life is dominated by cultural alignment.

How Systems Operate Through algorithmic processes, social identity is reinforced. Taking a neutral stance is often perceived as a lack of commitment or as a sidestepping of the issue at hand.

What Daily Life Feels Like Groups have an aura of security which may be more imagined than real. They also, however, present pressures to keep up.

Implications for Customers and Brands In this world, identity becomes an important infrastructure.

Belonging doesn't only provide emotional comfort, it provides access, validation, even protection. Neutrality is often interpreted as avoidance and that makes it really hard for brands to be allowed into the inner circles of customers. What people buy is shaped by cultural alignment and trust.

Value alignment is more important for decision-making than the superiority of the product or the legacy of the brand. An offer that looks strong on the surface can easily be rejected if there is lack of congruence with the expected norms in a particular group.

The trust shifts. It moves from believing a specific institution to trusting the narrative and experience of the community. Peer-to-peer validation is very important, more important than expert or celebrity endorsements. Scale doesn't matter as much as cultural relevance.

For brands, this environment can be either powerful or unforgiving!

Aligning closely with specific communities can build immense loyalty and generate advocacy. But one misstep, one opportunistic move and lack of authenticity can lead to a backlash and irreversible damage.

The strategic questions change:

- Which communities are we truly built to serve and ready to align to?
- Are we willing to accept the trade-offs?
- Are we authentic in our communication and does this external reality match our internal workings?

This is a future where it's more important to be trusted by the right people, because being liked by everyone proves impossible.

Future 4: Managed Scarcity

What the World Feels Like Constrained but purposeful. Within limits, restrictions are accepted, even expected.

How Systems Operate Various regulatory measures are put in place in order to prevent excessive use of resources. Investors regard a well-managed company as a better prospect than a similarly priced, less well run one.

What Daily Life Feels Like The implications of a decision are clear-cut. Choices are serious and carry long-term effects.

Implications for Customers and Brands Whether driven by regulation, economic rigour or environmental pressures — choices always come with consequences. In this world it is clear that there is scarcity. There is intentional unconsumption and trade-offs. To avoid collapse, this world is regulated and shaped by limits.

The shifts for customers are:

- Purchasing less, but being a lot more intentional about it. Durability, repairability, long-term value and function matter a lot more than aesthetics or novelty. Waste is frowned upon and irresponsible.
- Status is projected through responsibility, not possession or convenience. Speed gives way to efficient and careful use of resources.
- Impact is a key parameter people monitor and evaluate brands on.

And that changes the growth logic for brands. Volume is no longer the right metric and 'growth' is even regarded negatively. Long-term contribution and integration with the community is expected instead of short-term ROI spikes.

The strategic questions to be asked in this future are:

- Are we building for longevity or producing ongoing churn?
- What needs to change for us to remain successful in a world where people simply buy less?
- Can we still grow if we have to ensure we strengthen stability?

Legitimacy and responsibility go hand in hand in this future.

Reflection Point Even if the surface details in these four futures differ, the common trait here is that each world reshuffles which human needs move to the forefront. This is especially evident if the needs are evaluated through the lens of a specific product or service a company offers. In one future, agency almost disappears. In another, trust has to be repeatedly

STEP 01 - FUTURE LIVING ENVIRONMENT MAP			
FUTURE 01	FUTURE 02	FUTURE 03	FUTURE 04
Name Your Future	*Name Your Future*	*Name Your Future*	*Name Your Future*
What the world feels like?	*What the world feels like?*	*What the world feels like?*	*What the world feels like?*
How systems operate?	*How systems operate?*	*How systems operate?*	*How systems operate?*
What daily life feels like?	*What daily life feels like?*	*What daily life feels like?*	*What daily life feels like?*
What are the Implications for Customers and Brands?	*What are the Implications for Customers and Brands?*	*What are the Implications for Customers and Brands?*	*What are the Implications for Customers and Brands?*
Who primarily makes choices, sets constraints or absorbs consequences in this future context? ☐ *Individual* ☐ *Institutions / systems* ☐ *Distributed / hybrid*	*Who primarily makes choices, sets constraints or absorbs consequences in this future context?* ☐ *Individual* ☐ *Institutions / systems* ☐ *Distributed / hybrid*	*Who primarily makes choices, sets constraints or absorbs consequences in this future context?* ☐ *Individual* ☐ *Institutions / systems* ☐ *Distributed / hybrid*	*Who primarily makes choices, sets constraints or absorbs consequences in this future context?* ☐ *Individual* ☐ *Institutions / systems* ☐ *Distributed / hybrid*

Figure 4.2 Future Living Environment Map. Step 1.

earned and re-earned. In the third, belonging becomes important, and in the fourth, convenience gives way to responsibility. Now beware, you are not here to pick one of these four futures. You are here to observe how reality changes and how your relevance as a brand might increase or fade. So it would be wise to look beyond the trends and dig deeper into the needs and their shifts. In doing so, you can identify the non-negotiables for people in futures under pressure.

Step 2 — Prioritize Human Needs

Based on the needs synthesized from Maslow,[9] the Capability Approach,[10,11] Self-Determination Theory[12] and the needs of Max-Neef,[13] consider the following anchor set of human needs (see Figure 4.3):

- Safety & security
- Control & autonomy
- Trust & fairness
- Belonging & identity
- Competence & confidence
- Meaning & purpose
- Convenience & efficiency

For each future, answer:

If your customer lived in this world, which three needs would they need to protect above all others?

Exactly three.

This forced choice is the core of the Lab.

You should resist the temptation to select four or five. Or to argue that it depends.

This exercise works exactly because it takes away the comfort. If you think everything matters, then this means nothing is guiding the decision-making. You are forced to face the trade-offs by being constrained to choose only three needs.

You may find that the needs you selected are different in the four future contexts. This is to be expected and the point is not consistency but awareness.

My advice is, don't overthink it. Instead, capture the instinctive response first. You can always refine it in the following steps. And remember, what you are mapping is not preference, it's pressure.

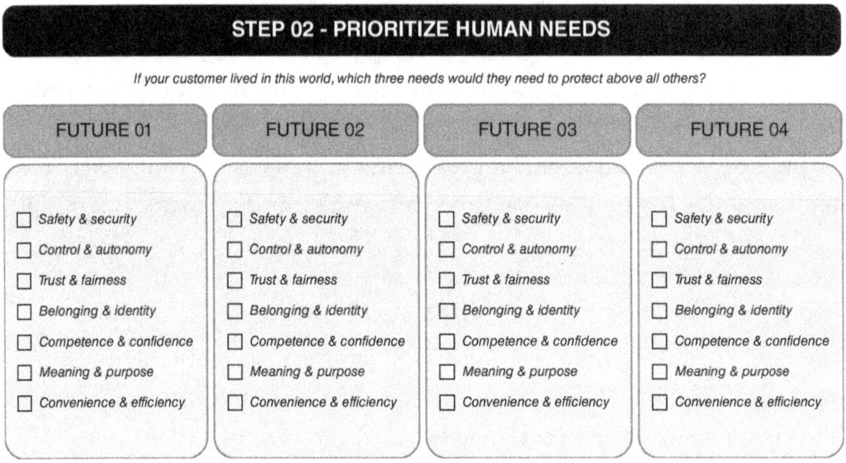

Figure 4.3 Future Living Environment Map. Step 2.

Step 3 — Create a Future Persona

A persona emerges from the prioritized needs. Create one or more personas for each future (see Figure 4.4).

Future: Frictionless but Opaque In this future, many everyday choices are no longer made by individuals. They are made by AI systems acting on people's behalf — selecting, filtering and prioritizing options at scale.

Persona name: AURA — Optimizing Agent — An AI Choosing on Behalf of People

What it is: an AI decision system trained to optimize outcomes across speed, cost and risk for large populations.

Top three needs it must satisfy (on behalf of humans):

1. Trust & fairness
2. Safety & security
3. Convenience & efficiency

Where agency sits: system-led.

AURA does not understand loyalty, symbolism or aspiration unless these are translated into tangible, measurable signals. It prioritizes what can be verified and ranked. Brand heritage, storytelling or cultural meaning do not matter, unless they show up as data points in performance, risk or reliability metrics.

Core tension: optimization vs human intent.

Human needs are increasingly filtered through non-human decision-makers, as algorithmic systems mediate choice, prioritization and access across markets and institutions.[14]

Future: Managed Scarcity

Persona Name: Elena – The Deliberate Minimalist

Age: 34

City: Barcelona

Top three needs:

1. Meaning & purpose
2. Safety & security
3. Competence & confidence

Elena is following the trend of conscious unconsumption and has reduced her purchasing to essentials. She researches durability scores before buying anything and subscribes to long-term repair programs instead of replacing items. She distrusts brands that rely on novelty. She wants fewer, better things that she can trust to last. What matters to her is longevity, transparency of sourcing and clear contribution to social stability.

Tension: she wants reliability without overconsumption. Brands that equate growth with volume feel misaligned with her reality. She rejects brands that disguise rapid replacement cycles as innovation.

Strategic Implication: if your category depends on repeat replacement cycles, this persona represents structural risk.

STEP 03 - CREATE A FUTURE PERSONA

Create one or more personas for each future.

FUTURE 01	FUTURE 02	FUTURE 03	FUTURE 04
Persona Name:	*Persona Name:*	*Persona Name:*	*Persona Name:*
About Persona:	*About Persona:*	*About Persona:*	*About Persona:*
Top three needs it must satisfy:	*Top three needs it must satisfy:*	*Top three needs it must satisfy:*	*Top three needs it must satisfy:*
Core Tension:	*Core Tension:*	*Core Tension:*	*Core Tension:*
Strategic Implication:	*Strategic Implication:*	*Strategic Implication:*	*Strategic Implication:*

Figure 4.4 Future Living Environment Map. Step 3.

Company: mid-sized regional banking group
Time horizon: 3–5 years

It's the strategy offsite of this banking group and the leadership team runs this Lab together.

Their performance is stable, but automation is accelerating and public scrutiny is rising. Therefore, the team wants to make sure they take action to prevent loss of market positioning. No crisis, yet. Exactly the right time to run the exercise.

Future 1: Frictionless but Opaque

Implications for the bank: Launch of automated financial advisors manage savings, loans and investments by default. It is rare for customers to choose products themselves.

Top three identified customer needs:

1. Trust & fairness
2. Control & autonomy
3. Convenience & efficiency

Persona: Maya — The Delegator

She uses automated financial tools to manage her savings and investments. Most of the time she rarely questions the system's recommendations until something unexpected happens. She heavily relies on them and appreciates the convenience. However, she is quietly starting to question whether the system truly serves her best interest.

Tension: banks are rarely trusted and now, when the algorithms choose products the tension is even higher. What she wants most is reassurance that the system is acting in her interest, not simply optimizing profit for someone else.

How does the bank prove it is acting in the customer's best interest? How does it ensure objectivity and non-discrimination?

Future 2: High Friction, Low Trust

Implications for the bank: institutions are scrutinized heavily with fees, lending practices and the bonuses of the executive teams publicly discussed and dissected.

Top three identified customer needs:

1. Safety & security
2. Trust & fairness
3. Competence & confidence

(continued)

(continued)

Persona: Arjun — The Verifier

He double-checks fees, compares lending terms publicly and questions inconsistencies. This behaviour is not a hobby but a response to repeated experiences where institutions failed to be transparent. He doesn't rely on institutional credibility. He spent months educating himself and he trusts only what he can independently validate. The brands he trusts are the ones that make it easy for him to verify their claims independently.

Tension: customers don't believe what the bank says. Compliance with regulations is not enough, customers only trust what they can verify.

Future 3: Identity & Belonging First

Implications for the bank: customers increasingly choose to work with banks that reflect their values. They support local and ethical investment and community funding practices.

Top three identified customer needs:

1. Belonging & identity
2. Meaning & purpose
3. Trust & fairness

Persona: Sofia — The Ethical Investor

Sofia wants her choices to reflect her deep values, that includes her money, which she insists has to reflect her social and cultural beliefs. The choices she makes take time. She often turns to communities and trusted networks to validate whether a brand's claims are genuine. She researches and makes a decision to partner with financial institutions that best align.

Tension: the traditional banking model and products feel outdated. You can't stay neutral in this context, you have to stand for something explicitly, even if this polarizes people. Brands that attempt to remain neutral or vague quickly lose her trust.

Future 4: Managed Scarcity

Implications for the bank: capital allocation is regulated extremely tightly. Lending portfolios are scored for environmental and social impact.

Top three identified customer needs:

1. Safety & security
2. Meaning & purpose
3. Competence & confidence

Persona: Wei — The Responsible Planner

Wei's decisions are based on responsible capital allocation. He would trade short-term gains for long-term stability and moderate returns if the financial institution proves transparency and sustainable impact.

Tension: growth and responsibility must go hand in hand.

Tier Logic

Trust & fairness appears in all four futures.

The team classifies it as Tier 1 – structural.

Convenience appears only once → Tier 2.

Belonging arises in only one of the futures, but it carries reputational risk if ignored → treated as existential signal.

Based on the needs, the following relevance areas were identified

1. Radical transparency in AI-driven financial decisions
2. Community-aligned lending strategy
3. Public impact scoring and disclosure

Decision Posture

After discussion, the team chooses to adjust.

They keep their core business model, but they make commitments to:

- Making algorithmic decision processes humanized and explainable.
- Publishing an annual lending impact report to ensure transparency.
- Introducing opt-in 'community allocation' savings products.

(*continued*)

(continued)

Consequence

Short Term: higher operational complexity and internal resistance.
Medium Term: stronger relevance across multiple plausible futures.

The team records in the Futures Strategy Canvas:

Tier 1 need	→	Trust & fairness
Decision posture	→	Adjust
Primary relevance arena	→	Transparent decision infrastructure

Step 4 — Prioritize Common Needs

Once all personas are created, compare needs across futures (see Figure 4.5).

Needs appearing in the top three repeatedly → Tier 1 (structural relevance).

Needs appearing only once → Tier 2 (contingent signals).

This distinction matters more than any single future.

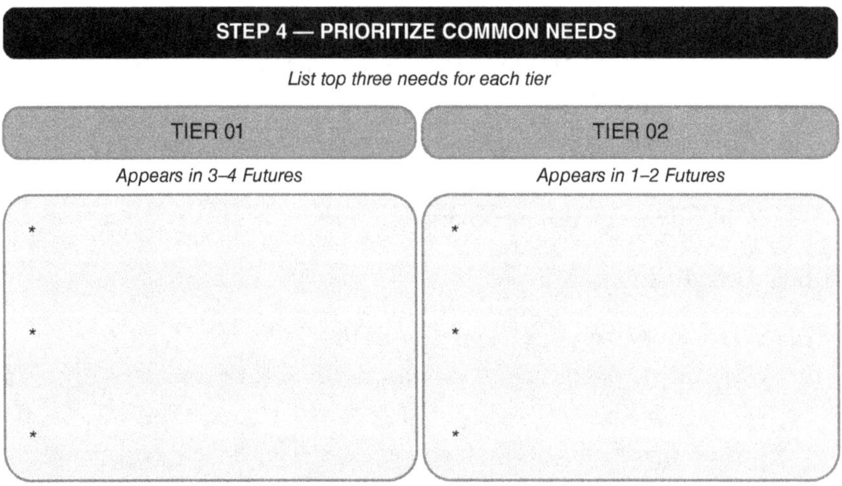

Figure 4.5 Future Living Environment Map. Step 4.

Step 5 — Barriers, Solutions and Organizational Advantage

For each Tier 1 and Tier 2 need, answer (see Figure 4.6):

- What makes this need harder to satisfy in the future?
  (loss of agency, opacity, regulation, scarcity, overload)
- What kinds of solutions might emerge — regardless of provider?
  (products, platforms, rules, intermediaries)
- Where does our organization have unfair advantage and could play?
  (assets, trust, capabilities, legitimacy, brand position)

When I am talking about unfair advantage, I don't mean rankings and scale. These are the assets your organization has that (a) remain true when pressure hits, and, (b) are hard to imitate by others.

Here are some questions you can ask yourselves to determine what the advantage is:

- **What do we have access to that others depend on?**
  (distribution networks, platforms, proprietary data, infrastructure, partnerships)
- **Where do we have permission to operate that others don't?**
  (cultural credibility, regulatory trust, community endorsement, brand legitimacy)
- **What capabilities would take competitors years, not months, to replicate?**
  (deep expertise, supply chain architecture, IP, talent density, long-term relational capital)
- **Where have we already proven credible under scrutiny or constraint?**
  (crisis response, regulatory review, public pressure, volatility)

Add one final discipline test:

- **If we had to operate here with half the budget, would we still have a defensible right to play?**
  If not, this is not a structural advantage, it is an aspiration.

Only when a future-critical need intersects with a real structural advantage does it qualify as a relevance arena.

It is only at this point that commercial potential and brand strategy enter the frame.

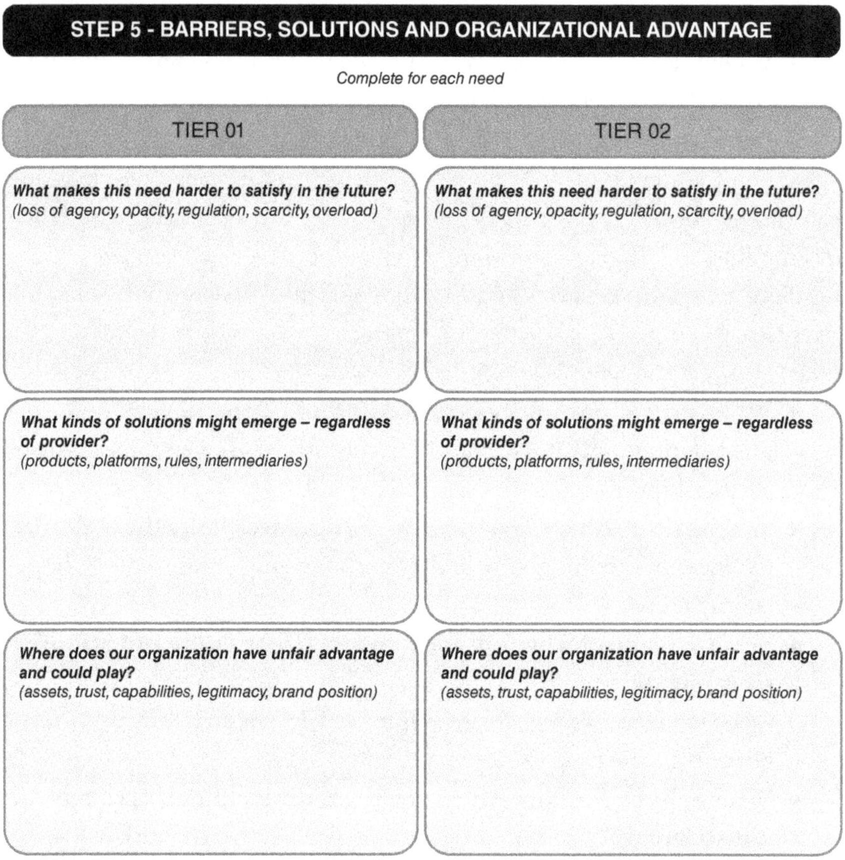

Figure 4.6 Future Living Environment Map. Step 5.

Step 6 — Define Future Relevance Arenas

Defining your future relevance arenas is important, because from these, you can work out what capabilities you may need in the future, in addition to what products and services you can launch (see Figure 4.7).

Capture three relevance arenas using this structure:

> **Supporting *[people or systems]* to achieve *[future-critical need]* in a world where *[specific future condition]*.**

For example: supporting customers to understand and influence automated financial decisions in a world where algorithms increasingly act on their behalf.

These are strategic commitments, not ideas.

Choose Your Strategic Posture You have three possible postures, you have to choose one:

Defend: protect and optimize your current core segment.
Short-term performance remains stable. Risk accumulates if structural needs shift faster than expected.

Adjust: maintain the core while deliberately investing in an emerging future segment.
Complexity increases, but optionality grows.

Reallocate: shift primary attention and investment toward a future-aligned segment.
Short-term volatility is likely. Long-term alignment may strengthen resilience.

Indecision is not neutral. It defaults to defending the present.

Choose your posture.

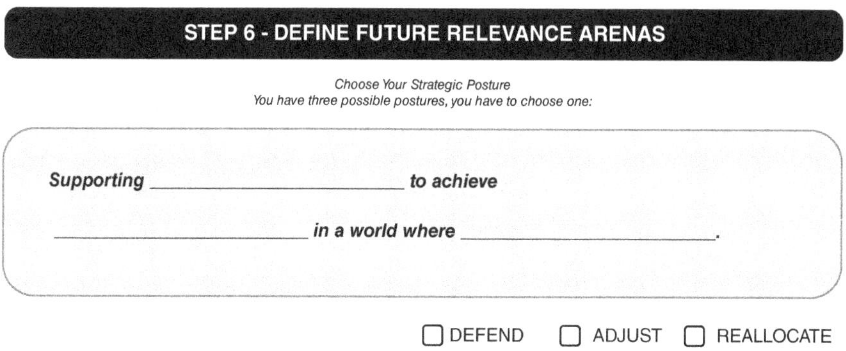

Figure 4.7 Future Living Environment Map. Step 6.

This is what moves into your Futures Strategy Canvas.

Why This Matters Beyond Marketing Identifying the future customer is not a brand exercise. It actually helps reshape (see Figure 4.8):

- Which products remain relevant.
- Which innovation bets deserve attention.
- Which external forces demand response.
- And ultimately, which strategic posture you adopt.

The customer lens becomes the pressure test for the entire strategy. If your defined future customers do not require your core offering, or require it in a different form, this impacts portfolio decisions, innovation allocation and even governance.

This Lab informs Labs 2, 4 and 5 directly.

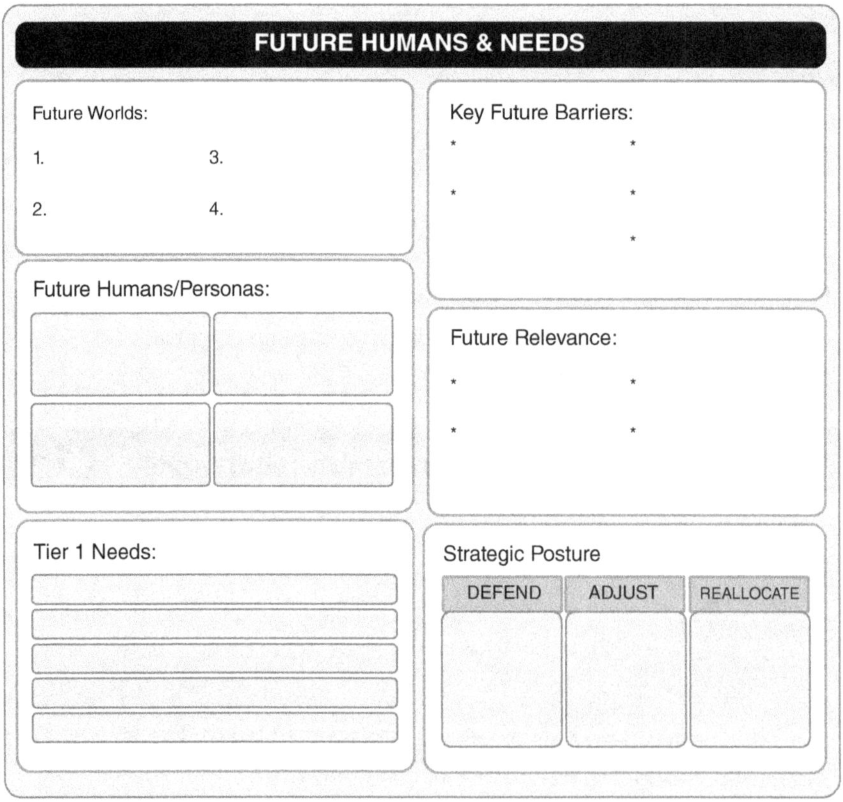

Figure 4.8 What You Carry Forward: Into the Futures Strategy Canvas.

What Goes into the Futures Strategy Canvas

From this Lab, record:

- Future world names
- Future personas (label, agency, tension)
- Tier 1 needs
- Key future barriers
- Future relevance arenas for your organization
- Strategic posture

Continue Your Strategic Path

This Lab focused on the future customer, who they might become and which needs rise under pressure.

If your next question is about whether your product will be relevant in the future, continue to **Strategic Futures Lab 2**.

If uncertainty sits around the future risks and opportunities you should be thinking about today, move to **Strategic Futures Lab 3**.

If the tension you feel relates to innovation, go to **Strategic Futures Lab 4**.

If you want to know whether your current strategy will remain resilient in the future, work through **Strategic Futures Lab 5**.

Each Lab stands alone and they don't have to be completed in any particular order.

This is meant to be a choose-your-own-path playbook and you should follow the tension that feels most relevant for your organization.

If strategy is rarely linear, then your path through this book shouldn't have to be either.

5 Strategic Futures Lab 2: Will My Product Still Be Relevant?

Tool: The Future Relevance Assessment

Products often lose relevance before they start losing revenue, and by then, your list of options has already shrunk. This Strategic Futures Lab forces the conversation while you still have room to manoeuvre.

Meet Your Future Self — Your POV

You have recently joined a new successfully growing company as head of portfolio. The company offers both digital services and digital and physical products.

It's that time of year again, when the new portfolio strategy is being reviewed. You are kicking off the portfolio strategy planning process with your very capable teams. The first in-person workshop in a while is coming up and you have asked everyone to come prepared with the information they are responsible for.

They are not expecting the process to look too different than any other year. There is an overall company growth percentage number that gets generated mainly based on past performance and existing internal data and ambitions. Revenue seems stable, customers are still buying, the roadmap is full.

However, you notice a few worrying facts:

- External information is not taken into account when decisions are being made.
- There are strong leadership opinions and preferences toward certain products and services.
- There seems to be a dependency on a few large customers who still buy, but two of the contracts are due to be renegotiated in a year.
- The portfolio has seen no exits in the past and has remained largely unchanged.
- The innovation pipeline seems driven by internal motivators and has not considered potential shifts in regulation that may come as a second or third order implication of emerging social trends.

Nothing is obviously broken — yet. But a looming worry sits within you and you wonder, are we very good at serving the present but solving for a problem that might not matter in the future?

It's not anxiety about disruption and sudden failure, but a concern about something much more dangerous — slow relevance decay.

Products may lose relevance before they lose revenue. This aligns with McGrath's (2013) argument that traditional performance metrics are lagging indicators, often delaying recognition of shifts in relevance.[1] By the time you spot the decline in your financial metrics, the list of strategic options tends to be shorter.

This Lab is here to force a timely decision.

It's always harder to defend action when things aren't failing loudly. It feels uncomfortable to shake the status quo, especially when things are moving along.

If the revenue was decreasing, if customers were switching to another brand, if another company had launched a radically better service you would have permission to act. The decision would be urgent and you would have an invisible enemy to fight. But now, performance is stable and nobody expects stability to be dangerous.

But deep down, you can sense that everything in the portfolio is always optimized for continuity and not change.

The same core assumptions. The same growth logic. The same product categories — the mantra has been 'let's repeat and do more of what already works'. Each year, it's the same narrative but refined, extended, improved and never really questioned.

Something is unsettling. Looking at the portfolio it isn't clear which products or product groups could prove they are resilient in a different future, which ones are just riding inertia and which ones would collapse at the smallest customer shift.

Some of these products look very strong today. However they are dependent on conditions that are shifting:

- Route to market models that might be disrupted.
- Customer behaviours that may fragment.
- Regulatory freedoms that may cease to exist.

You have tried to recommend phasing out but each product group has a champion and teams that are built around them, careers tied to their success and frankly, letting go of something that still shows some form of performance might seem reckless and definitely feels irrational.

But you know the facts: if the numbers are already declining, this means the options have already shrunk and before you know it, repositioning becomes a lot less strategic and a lot more defensive. Talent switches priorities and companies. Margins quickly threaten to disappear.

This Lab is here to help you make decisions while you still have enough room to Manoeuvre and help you avoid being cornered.

The Leadership Question

Which of our current products/product groups and services will remain relevant in the future, which must adapt and which should no longer anchor our strategy?

We are not looking to solve innovation here. We are not going to build a roadmap — Futures Lab 4 is the one that can help with mapping future-relevant innovation opportunities. We aren't going to do a performance review here either.

In this Lab we will focus on taking decisions about our portfolio to ensure its future relevance.

Why Existing Tools Fall Short for This Question

Most leadership teams already use a range of well-established tools to manage products and portfolios. Many of them are effective, they are just not designed to answer this future-anchored question.

Portfolio tools such as the BCG Growth–Share Matrix help allocate resources within established markets, but are not designed to determine whether a product's underlying value will remain relevant as human needs, culture and the context within which decisions are being taken, change.[2]

The Jobs To Be Done framework, popularized by Clayton Christensen, usefully shifts focus from products to underlying human motivations. However, it is primarily a present-state design tool. It assumes relative stability in context, agency and constraints. When those conditions change — through automation, platformization or regulation — the 'job' may persist while its meaning and satisfiers change dramatically.[3]

Roadmaps and lifecycle models are essential for execution, but are structurally backward-looking. They rely on historical data, known users and existing incentives.

Finally, scenario planning and strategic wind tunnelling (used later in this book) are powerful for testing overall strategy, but too heavy for the more immediate, earlier decision leaders must make to answer the question:

Does this product or product group deserve to be carried forward into the future at all?

While elements of this question appear across strategy, innovation and foresight tools, I have not found any that are designed to help leaders explicitly decide what should no longer anchor the future before decisions are forced by decline.

This Lab exists to address that.

What This Tool Is (and Is Not)

The Future Relevance Assessment is a proprietary tool I am introducing in this book.

I've designed it to help leaders make one of three explicit decisions about an existing product or service:

- **Protect:** this is a future-safe bet.
- **Adapt:** the need persists, but the offering must change.
- **Phase out:** the product should no longer anchor future strategy.

It does not:

- Predict demand.
- Generate solutions.
- Redesign products.

The output from this Lab should not be simply insights. It should lead to commitment.

The Future Context for This Lab

This is a choose-your-own-path book, so I am not going to assume you have started at Strategic Futures Lab 1, but in case you have, feel free to bring forward:

- The future contexts or scenarios you worked with.
- The priority human needs you identified.

If you have not done that yet, simply use the shared future context below to complete the exercise.

You are not asked to create futures in this Lab, but to make decisions under plausible future pressure.

Shared Future Context

Assume a future where:

Trust is much harder to earn and much easier to lose. Some simple decisions are often outsourced to technology to mediate or automate. Efficiency and resilience are both expected as a bare minimum. And people are very sensitive to legitimacy, transparency and agency.

This framing is consistent with current futures research on socio-technical transitions and decision environments.[4,5]

If you struggle with weighting the different disruptions, you can apply a simple logical filter:

- Does this shift alter who satisfies the need?
- Does it change where agency sits?
- Does it introduce a new barrier to satisfaction?
- Does it reduce your structural advantage?

The more 'yes' answers you give here, the more material the disruption is to your product relevance.

Anchor Set: Human Needs

To avoid vague discussion, this Lab works from an explicit set of human needs, synthesized from established research rather than invented here.

This approach reflects a long-standing consensus in behavioural and development theory: core human needs remain relatively stable, while the conditions under which they are fulfilled change.[6,7]

This Lab is not asking you to redefine needs. Instead it asks you to decide which ones matter the most under the provided future conditions.

To make this exercise more relevant, I encourage you to hack the tool so that it serves you best. The logic to follow is the same, but you can be as specific as possible about the needs (or wants) that your product or service addresses.

How This Lab Works

1. Identify the core human needs your product serves today.
2. Reframe those needs under future pressure.
3. Identify new barriers or alternative satisfiers.
4. Make a protect/adapt/phase-out decision.
5. Write down the assumptions that must remain true.

This is not product design but portfolio governance.

Step 1 — Select the Three Needs This Product Serves

For the product, product group or service in focus, choose up to three human needs it genuinely supports today (see Figure 5.1). Make sure you are not discussing the product features or its benefits, but the real human need in today's world that your offering satisfies.

Product adoption is often shaped by how well offerings match users' expectations and mental models.[8]

Be honest and disciplined, because internal narratives and over-claiming can hide fragility.

FUTURE RELEVANCE ASSESSMENT

(Decide: PROTECT / ADAPT / PHASE OUT)

PRODUCT / SERVICE:

FUTURE CONTEXT USED: ☐ Provided baseline ☐ Our scenarios

STEP 1 — SELECT THE THREE NEEDS THIS PRODUCT SERVES

(pick up to 3)

- ☐ *Safety & security*
- ☐ *Competence & confidence*
- ☐ *Control & autonomy*
- ☐ *Meaning & purpose*
- ☐ *Trust & fairness*
- ☐ *Convenience & efficiency*
- ☐ *Belonging & identity*

NOTES: *What outcome this need enables for the user*

Figure 5.1 Future Relevance Assessment. Step 1.

Step 2 — Reframe Those Needs in the Future Context

Now that you have identified these needs, place them into the assumed future context (see Figure 5.2). You can refer to Strategic Lab 1 for four sample future scenarios or work with your own.

For each need ask the question:

- Does this need still exist, does its importance grow or does it lose priority? Does it collide with other needs?
- Does its meaning change in any way under automation, regulation or social pressure?
- Who primarily satisfies this need in the future: a human, a brand, a system, a platform or an AI agent?

This step distinguishes enduring need from context-specific satisfaction — a critical strategic distinction.[9]

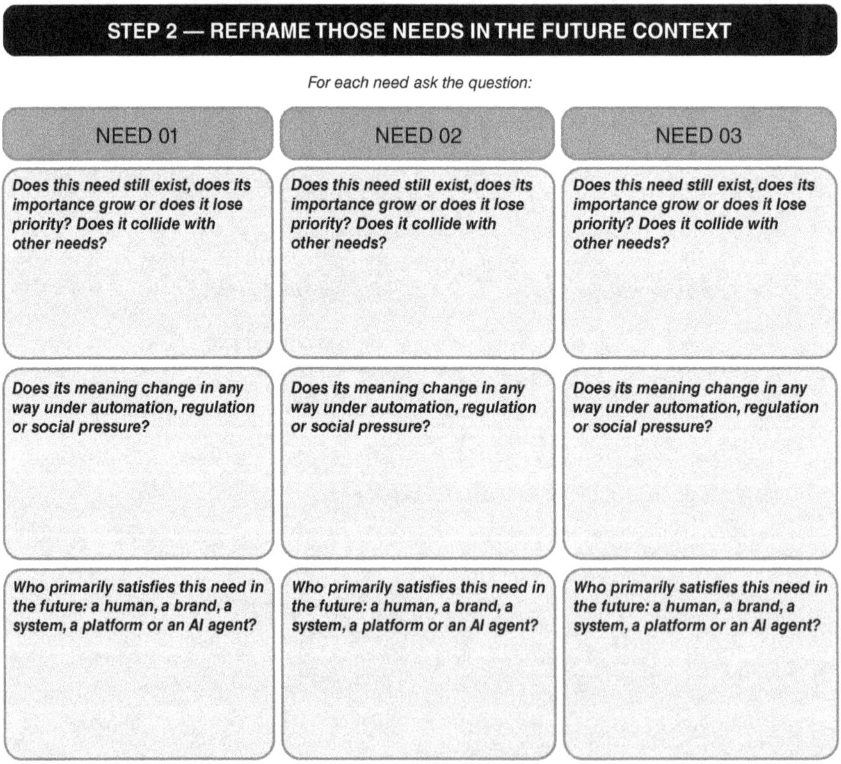

Figure 5.2 Future Relevance Assessment. Step 2.

Step 3 — Identify Future Barriers

We can assume that needs rarely disappear, but their priority changes and the relevance of a brand, service or product could disappear when barriers to satisfying the need change (see Figure 5.3).

For each need, ask:

- What new barriers prevent this need from being met?
- What frictions increase? (complexity, mistrust, loss of agency).
- What alternative solutions, from any actor, could satisfy this need better?

This reflects systems thinking work showing that shifts in constraints matter more than shifts in preference.[10]

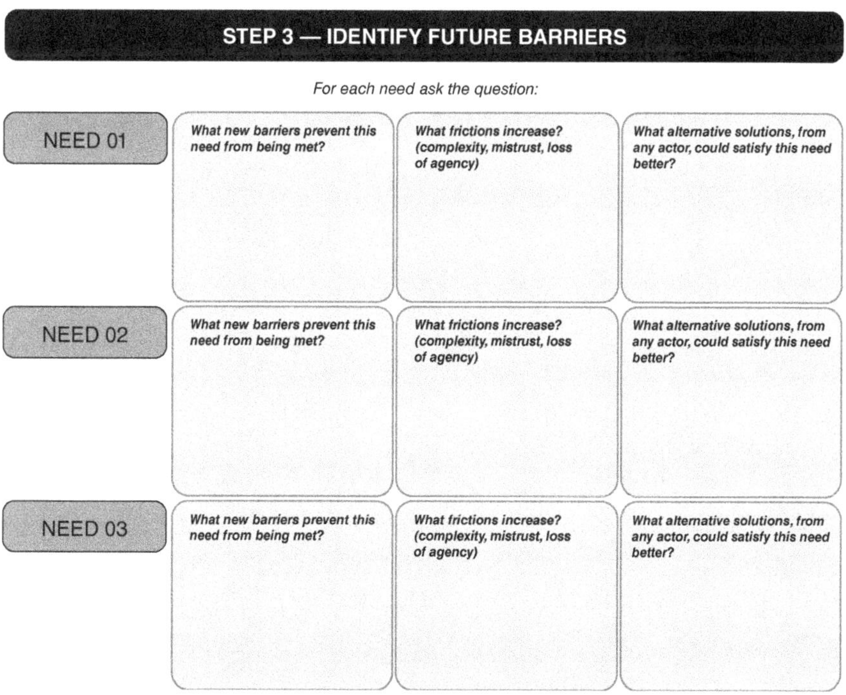

Figure 5.3 Future Relevance Assessment. Step 3.

Step 4 — Make the Relevance Decision

Decision time!

It's time to think through the services and products and categorize them into one of these three categories (see Figure 5.4):

Protect (Safe Bet)

Supports needs that remain structurally important across futures, with a value logic that still holds.

Adapt

This reflects a need that persists, but requires significant change to remain relevant.

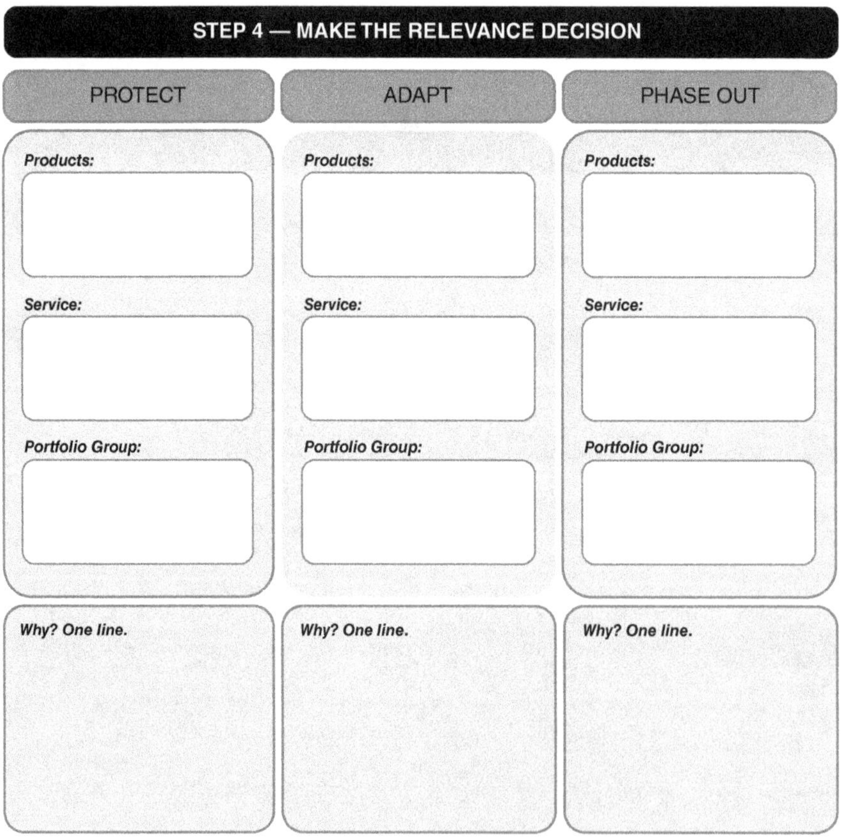

Figure 5.4 Future Relevance Assessment. Step 4.

Phase Out

The product's core value weakens, becomes indirect, or is likely to be better satisfied elsewhere.

No neutral option is allowed here, a choice must be made. Indecision is itself a decision to leave our future success to chance.

What Your Decision Sets in Motion

In a true choose-your-own-path manner, each choice leads to a certain outcome and it comes with a set of trade-offs. We should, however, adopt the mindset of being flexible and I would always advise continuing to monitor the signals that can indicate whether our assumptions were right or not. Then, at each irreversible decision point, make sure we run the exercise and have the most up-to-date information to work with.

Let's look at the possible consequences of your choices here:

When you choose Protect, Adapt or Phase Out you make a commitment. Each choice changes the shape of your portfolio risk over time.

Choosing Protect Means

Short Term (0–12 Months) Continuity feels reassuring, especially when revenue holds, teams feel justified and momentum continues. This really looks like the safest choice, where:

- Performance is stable.
- Focus on operations remains undisrupted.
- Internally there is peace and alignment.

Mid Term (1–3 Years) Signals may start appearing and weaken assumptions. Customer expectations shift quietly, the differentiating factor in your product or service may become a standard, which means losing advantage. This means:

- Margins start to shrink.
- Marketing costs increase simply because you have to defend relevance.
- Product updates become reactive rather than strategic.

Long Term (3–5+ Years) If the foundational customer need has shifted, the product no longer anchors in the future. It remains lingering in the portfolio, where it swallows resources but offers less and less leverage when it comes to growth opportunities. As a result:

- Strategic options become less available.
- Repositioning becomes defensive and not proactively shaping a desirable future.
- Exiting becomes more expensive than it would have been earlier.

Choosing Protect is not wrong, of course, but you have to know that you are making a bet that stability will last longer than uncertainty.

Choosing Adapt Means

Short Term (0–12 Months) This feels uncomfortable and slightly too ambiguous. Teams are stretched and need convincing. Investment rises, yet no results are visible for the time being. Complexity increases and many are questioning the decision. You may experience:

- Temporary margin pressure.
- Organizational learning curve.
- Internal resistance from legacy champions.

Mid Term (1–3 Years) If your assumptions were correct, you will find that the product begins to fit emerging conditions better and you gain flexibility. You are actively engaged in change, have an advantage and are able to dictate some conditions. Teams feel empowered and supportive. Meanwhile, customers feel understood. As a result you have:

- Stronger market legitimacy.
- Increased optionality.
- Clearer positioning.

Long Term (3–5+ Years) If the team has done the job right, to create adaptation that is foundational and not simply cosmetic, the product becomes resilient. It evolves with the environment rather than fighting it. This leads to:

- Portfolio longevity.
- Lower risk of sudden disruption.
- Strategic breathing space.

When you choose Adapt, you are saying 'the problem doesn't disappear, but our current solution won't be enough'. It is still a bet, but it is a bet that the customer need will still be there, even though they will expect a different solution.

If You Choose Phase Out

Short Term (0–12 Months) Resistance surfaces immediately and it will be hard to defend, especially if revenue dips initially. The emotional attachment also becomes visible and you will be faced with resistance to change. This looks like:

- Internal pushback.
- Transitional instability.
- Short-term financial trade-off.

Mid Term (1–3 Years) When capital and talent are redeployed, clarity and focus increase and the portfolio sharpens, things start to settle. You'll likely see:

- Cleaner strategic narrative.
- Stronger allocation discipline.
- Increased innovation capacity.

Long Term (3–5+ Years) Risk exposure reduces and resources are anchored in areas aligned with future demand. As a result, you are more likely to have:

- Greater agility.
- Reduced legacy drag.
- Stronger structural positioning.

Phase Out is probably the hardest bet to take in the presence of no hard evidence, and that is why it is important to keep an eye on the external world and take informed decisions you won't regret. There is always a risk, it's like the stock market, but the more you practice this thought process, the greater clarity you will have on when to act and what signals to look for.

If you think that the neutral option is to not choose at all, then I have to say this is where the real risk lies. There is no safe option, only perceived safety and informed and conscious exposure.

This Lab exists so you choose that exposure deliberately and while you are in control and can prepare for the consequences, not reactively out of desperation.

Step 5 — State the Assumptions You Are Making

For each decision, write three to five explicit future-facing assumptions that must hold for it to be correct (see Figure 5.5). These are usually called 'signposts' in foresight. You can use these to create an early warning system. The agency or futurist doing horizon scanning for you could look out for signals that prove or disprove these assumptions and can communicate to you early enough when signals of change impact your portfolio hypotheses. This provides another practical use of foresight that doesn't depend on scenarios but is anchored into the everyday signal spotting.

Examples:

- People will continue to desire human oversight, they will not allow full automation.
- Trust will remain a differentiator, not a baseline expectation.
- Convenience will no longer outweigh legitimacy.

Explicit assumptions are critical for adaptive strategy and later monitoring.[11]

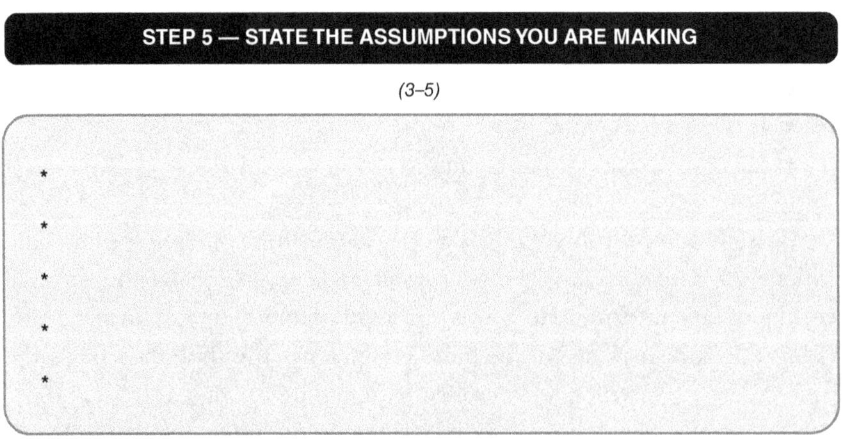

Figure 5.5 Future Relevance Assessment. Step 5.

Company: mid-sized B2B SaaS workflow platform
Time horizon: 3–5 years
Context: stable growth, strong corporate contracts, very low churn.

The leadership team runs this Lab during their annual portfolio review.

This company's top product represents 48% of total revenue generated. It is a workflow automation dashboard that large enterprises use to track reporting and team performance.

It looks untouchable and the plans are to invest more in upgrading some of its functionalities. But it's only untouchable on the surface. Let's see why.

Step 1: What Human Needs Does It Serve Today?

After a short debate, the team picks:

- Competence & confidence
- Convenience & efficiency
- Control & autonomy

They all agree (which is usually a warning sign in my mind!) that the product helps middle management feel capable, efficient and in control of team output. In addition, it helps leadership teams feel in control.

OK, so far, so good.

Step 2: Reframing in the Future Context

Let's now look at the shared future assumption:

- Trust is fragile
- Automation increases
- Legitimacy matters
- AI mediates decisions

The tension now becomes much clearer.

(*continued*)

(*continued*)

If AI begins automating reporting and decision logic: *where does 'control' sit? With managers or does it shift to systems?*

If dashboards are AI-generated summaries: *what happens to competence — does it increase or decrease?*

If employee surveillance and personal data protection concerns grow: *Are efficiency and legitimacy starting to clash?*

The team debate is starting to centre around a tension — the idea of the product was to help visibility and control, but if there is sensitivity around trust and fairness, visibility can feel like surveillance.

Step 3: Future Barriers

Several new barriers emerge:

- AI-native companies are offering predictive analytics instead of dashboards.
- Clients are consolidating vendors into integrated AI suites.
- Employee backlash against monitoring tools, demanding payment for their data or wanting to opt out completely.
- Regulations limiting performance-tracking data.

In reality, this product is now competing on philosophy, not just features. Assumption and confidence — dissembled.

Step 4: The Relevance Decision

At first all but one of the executives say 'Protect. This is our flagship!'

But after carefully mapping assumptions, they shift the decision to:

Adapt.

Why?

Because even though the needs for competence and efficiency are still there, the form of control has to change:

From surveillance → to empowerment and from tracking → to guidance.

Step 5: Explicit Assumptions

They record these assumptions:

1. Enterprises will continue valuing structured performance visibility.
2. AI will not completely replace human managerial judgement.
3. Compliance regulation will allow structured analytics if transparent.
4. Employees will accept monitoring if they see fairness and reciprocity.
5. Human oversight will remain desirable in automated environments.

They assign their foresight team to monitor signals in:

- Labour regulation
- AI workplace governance
- Enterprise AI platform consolidation
- Employee activism in tech-enabled monitoring

Outcome

This particular team does not completely redesign the product during this Lab exercise, but it commits to:

- Reframing product positioning around empowerment.
- Launching a transparency audit feature.
- Exploring AI augmentation rather than pure oversight.

And most critically they agree that one legacy reporting module will be phased out within 18 months if the signals indicate that the assumption about where the future is headed are confirmed. They commit to this action, even though at the moment this product still generates revenue.

Mini Example: Consumer Subscription Brand

Product: premium meal-kit subscription service.

Needs served today: convenience & efficiency, competence & confidence.

Future tension: if AI meal planners integrated in smart kitchens provide automated grocery delivery at optimized cost and nutrition, the 'meal-kit' becomes redundant.

Decision: Adapt. Shift from delivering ingredients toward delivering curated cultural experiences and skill-building components not easily automated.

What Goes into the Futures Strategy Canvas

From this Lab, record in the Futures Strategy Canvas (see Figure 5.6):

- Product, service or product group
- Three priority human needs
- Relevance decision (Protect/Adapt/Phase Out)
- Key future assumptions

You are not yet bringing solutions, initiatives and timelines to the table, just decisions on which category each product and service belongs to.

Why This Lab Matters

Without this step, organizations could fall in the trap of:

- Protecting products because they perform today and because they have emotional attachment to them or the status quo.
- Innovating around declining relevance.
- Or postponing difficult conversations until options have narrowed.

This Lab aims to prevent that drift.

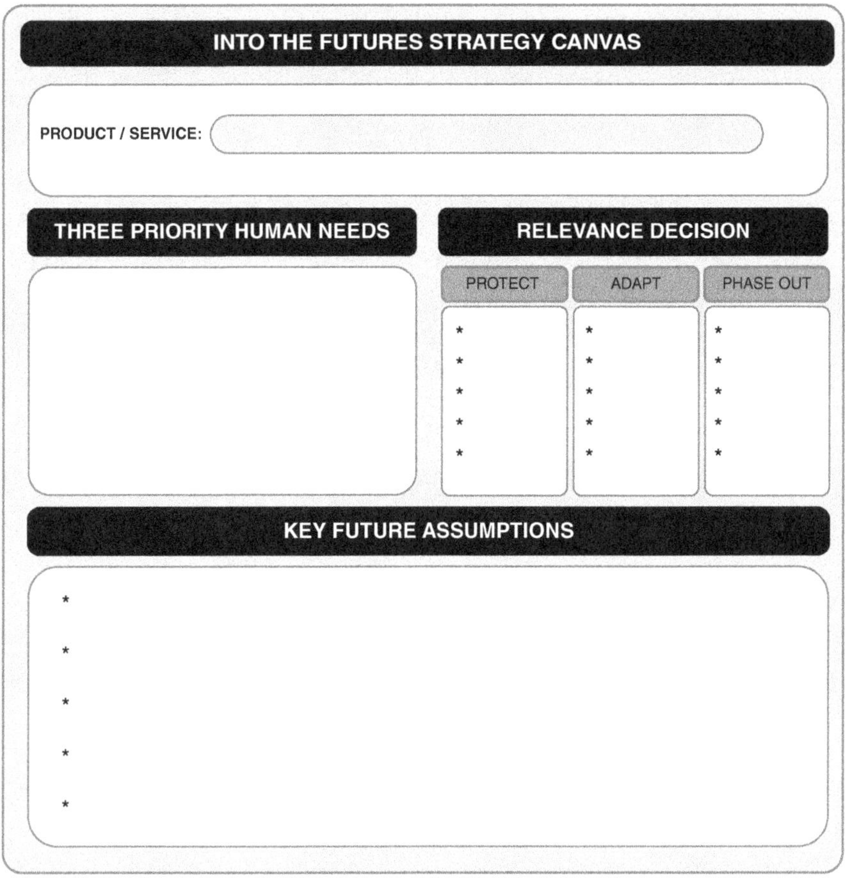

Figure 5.6 What You Carry Forward: Into the Futures Strategy Canvas.

Continue Your Strategic Path

This Lab focused on future product relevancy, what needs your product serves and how these might change under future scenarios. If your next question is about who your future customer might be, move to **Strategic Futures Lab 1**.

If uncertainty sits around the future risks and opportunities you should be thinking about today, continue to **Strategic Futures Lab 3**.

If the tension you feel relates to innovation, go to **Strategic Futures Lab 4**.

If you want to know whether your current strategy will remain resilient in the future go to **Strategic Futures Lab 5**.

Each Lab stands alone and they don't have to be completed in any particular order.

This is meant to be a choose-your-own-path playbook and you should follow the tension that feels most relevant for your organization.

6 Strategic Futures Lab 3: What Future Risks and Opportunities Require Decisions Now?

Tool: Strategic Decision Tree

This Strategic Futures Lab is about stepping outside the building, not looking inwards, because the biggest disruptions to your strategy rarely start inside your organization, or even your industry.

Meet Your Future Self — Your POV

You are in the executive meeting, five minutes early, chatting to a couple of your colleagues about the stock market. It has been shaky, clearly impacted by the political climate.

The Futurist you hired starts the presentation and you stare at the title slide while he is introducing himself: 'Top Trends that will impact 2035'.

There are 20 of them and everyone around the table has a different opinion on which one is more important than the others. The Head of Marketing generally thinks they are cultural noise. The CFO wants percentage probability and predictions so she can plan with certainty. The Head of Product wants to know which three he should latch on to so that he doesn't miss the next big shift. Meanwhile, the Head of Legal is warning about regulation that may cause serious implications for the business if these trends really materialize. The CEO finally says with a note of impatience: 'OK, it's great to know these trends, but so what? Which ones actually matter to our business and what should we be doing about it?'

You feel somewhat detached from this conversation, because 2035 seems too far away and following from the latest conversation with your team, you think it's not going to be easy to evaluate what the operating environment might look like.

This is the exact moment this Futures Lab is built for.

Because trends don't create outcomes, the decisions of the leadership team do.

And that is the part that bothers you more than you would like to admit, it just sits heavier than you expected.

It is easy to discuss and debate whether a trend is a fad, or whether it's real. Whether it is exaggerated or unlikely. It actually is a nice intellectual exercise that doesn't really help in this case, because it is a lot more difficult to acknowledge that even when you choose not to respond to a trend or to just ignore it because it feels uncomfortable, this is still a deliberate choice that leads to consequences, just like any other choice.

As the discussion unfolds, you begin to notice something very interesting — each team is interpreting the same trend list through its own lens and arguing their case.

Marketing is thinking about cultural relevance and brand perception. Finance is thinking about exposure and downside protection. Legal is looking for compliance risk. The product management team is scanning for every possible opportunity. No one is wrong, but no one is integrating the whole picture either. And that is the biggest opportunity here. This room doesn't lack intelligence, but it doesn't yet have the shared frame of responsibility that it needs to move forward in unison.

'Which trends actually matter to our business? What should we be doing about it?' the CEO asks again, a little more loudly. This question is not about predicting, it's about taking ownership, based on the information you all have. She isn't looking for another PowerPoint deck. She is trying to get an answer from her leadership team and a reassurance that her team can distinguish between noise and material exposure. She also wants to know whether this team is prepared to take responsibility for acting, and acting early enough to prevent decline or disruption. This is what strategic discussions should look like.

Maybe you came to this Lab thinking you would get predictions and ready answers, showing you what 2035 will look like. But the reality is this Lab is about deciding today where you are willing to commit, where you decide to prepare and where you are consciously choosing not to engage.

That clarity is what separates informed leadership from passive observation, even though this exercise might feel uncomfortable.

Remember, this team isn't lacking information and intelligence. They're drowning in it and requesting more, but what you really need is a way to turn all of these scattered external influences into a short, shared view of:

- What could impact your operating environment, how big is the risk?
- What could actually open a new opportunity?
- What are the things you can't ignore that require deliberate choices and actions now — not tomorrow, not in a year's time, not later?

The Discomfort You Shouldn't Ignore

Through my experience I have identified a pattern — when the business is successful, it's hard to convince the leaders that looking outside-in is worth it. Futures work is usually commissioned when there is a crisis — either drop in sales, or a major external disruption and uncertainty, and it is usually asked to deliver certainty.

When we already see that the world has shifted, leadership teams tend to do one of two things:

1. They monitor endlessly. This is when they start asking for more information in an attempt to monitor everything but quite often decide very little as a result.
2. They overreact. This means they take action, which is basically a reaction to the loudest trend that is obvious and established already and then call that futures strategy.

Both feel time consuming and can throw the research teams into working tirelessly, but neither brings actual clarity of the overall picture, nor does either bring intention, or preparedness for that matter.

You really don't need a longer trend list. What you do need is a disciplined and methodical way to answer a simple CEO question:

'What future risks and opportunities require decisions now?'

To get to the answer in a systematic way, let's take a look at what is really happening:

- You have external forces that are coming at you from all sides — Social, Technological, Economic, Environmental and Political, in addition to Values and Culture (STEEP + VC).
- There are Social (S) and Cultural (C) movements that rapidly define 'acceptable' behaviour for brands and employers, that reflect the changing societal Values (V).
- Tech shifts occur that may change customer expectations or create opportunities overnight.
- Economic and environmental factors arise that bring volatility, which in turn can vastly impact cost structure, supply chain and growth plans.
- Geopolitical fragmentation can reshuffle market access and talent flows.

If you are not monitoring all these, then I suggest you either develop an internal capability in foresight or find a good external partner who can advise you on these topics and their implications to your business. In many companies, however, the problem isn't the lack of information.

Trend reports are abundant, they can be sourced through various different channels, but they have two main problems:

1. They consist of trends — which means the shifts have happened already and you are seeing them unfold.
2. Everyone else is also seeing them, limiting your advantage.

That is why I advocate for a professionally trained and experienced foresight team or consultant, who performs horizon scanning and spots signals before they become trends.

The main issue is not finding the trends, it's knowing what steps to take so that your team can decide what to do about them. It's the informed, deliberate and methodical choices that will feed your strategy, whether you choose to react to trends or lead the trends towards the future.

You also have a team problem (again, not a data problem).

In most leadership rooms, different functions see very different futures:

- The Brand and Marketing team sees identity and cultural relevance.
- Finance sees risk and exposure.
- Operations sees constraints.
- Legal sees compliance and liability.
- The Product team sees opportunity and capability bets.
- The Innovation team sees opportunities.

If you don't force these perspectives into the same conversation, you don't get futures intelligence. Instead you get parallel monologues, which stifle decision-making.

This Lab forces a shared decision conversation. Not necessarily a consensus as a starting point, but definitely a more well-rounded perspective for everyone and clarity.

The Process: From Trend Noise → To Decision Clarity

This Lab has a two-step flow:

Step 1: filter what matters

Step 2: decide what it means

Most executive rooms don't struggle with information, but commitment.

When 30 trends are on the table, it almost feels required and responsible to monitor all of them, but watching trends is very different to actually taking a decision on what actions to take. The longer this decision is postponed, the longer the risk exposure.

In this Lab, I am not asking you to have 'the right' opinion on every single external force. I am inviting you to identify which forces are important enough to influence your path to success and big enough to require you to allocate resources, priorities and posture differently.

Making this selection and prioritization is uncomfortable, because you have to let go of some and decide they are not important to you, at least not now. This type of clarity brings focus and direction, which will support the resilience of the strategy.

Step 1 — Filter What Matters

Tool: Probability × Impact Matrix Reimagined by the Futures School

What It Is A simple way to take a messy set of trends, discuss and agree which ones are probable and impactful to the business. The matrix I'm introducing here has been modified by the Futures School to focus specifically on trend prioritization, rather than risk management, which is what other versions of this tool are intended for.[1]

What You Do Teams start with a set of trends.

First, they map them on a Probability × Impact Matrix (see Figure 6.1) to identify which trends are strategically important in the next five years and have to be addressed now.

Only the trends in the medium and high-impact + high-probability zone move forward.

These selected trends are then taken through a Strategic Decision Tree (see Figure 6.2), which helps leaders explore consequences, responsibilities and required choices.

The tools are sequential and visually connected: filter → decision.

Bring your trend list — 10, 20 items. It doesn't matter how many. What matters is that you plan this session as a workshop, attended by all of the key stakeholders I mentioned earlier, because you need them to discuss the implications of each of these trends on their area of responsibility. This will give you a holistic picture on what the possible implications for the business are.

As a first step, select a time horizon — five years is a good start. Then as a team, discuss the implications of each trend for the business and map them onto a matrix answering these questions:

Probability How likely is this trend to materialize and affect our operating environment in our strategic time horizon?

Impact If it happens, how big is the effect on our business model, category or ability to deliver?

Rules You are not trying to be correct. You can't accurately predict something that hasn't happened yet and has no hard evidence. You're trying to be aware of what might happen, how it may affect different parts of the business and, most importantly, to be aligned.

Don't argue 'true or false'. Argue if it is 'material or not'.

If people disagree, capture the topic — that disagreement is a signal. You can always look for more evidence or continue to monitor the development of this particular trend.

Output A short list of trends that land in the zone you define as strategically important — High probability × Medium + High Impact

Everything else gets consciously parked:

Zone 2 → include in future scenarios.

Zone 3 → create a mitigation plan for crisis situations.

Zone 4 → ignore for now, but keep an eye it doesn't move to medium impact.

That exercise alone reduces anxiety, informs the leadership team and gets them talking to each other. But it doesn't create decisions yet!

Step 2 — Strategic Decision Tree

Your decision tree is the bridge between 'this matters' and 'what do we do about it?'

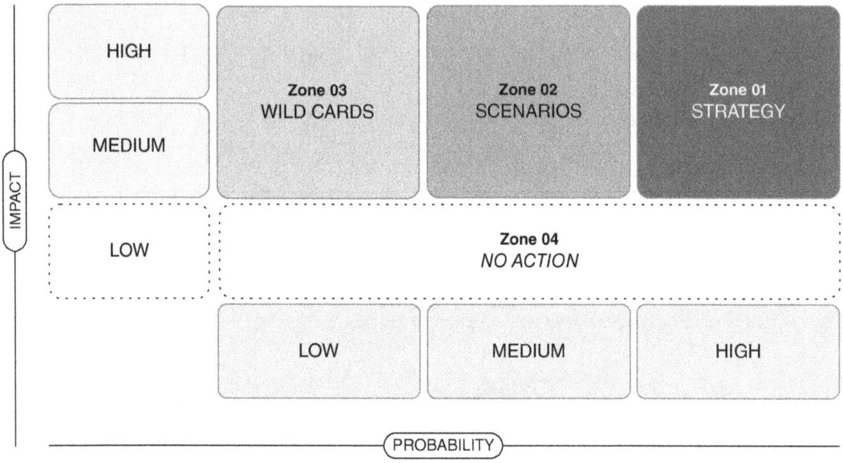

Figure 6.1 Probability x Impact Matrix.

What It Is

The Strategic Decision Tree moves us from simple awareness to action. It helps leadership teams turn important external forces into explicit choices, by asking three questions.

This tool does not predict the future, what it does is to make today's decision posture explicit.

For each important trend, it answers three questions:

1. Does this require a strategic decision from us?
2. What posture should we take right now?
3. Where are we already committed and where are we only aligned in theory?

What You Do

Take only the trends shortlisted in Step 1 (high probability × medium/high impact) and run them through the decision tree one at a time. Trends enter the decision tree in order of impact, starting with high-impact trends, followed by medium-impact ones.

For each trend, the facilitator walks the group through a fixed sequence of questions.

This can be done as part of the same workshop or it can be an automated process as part of a knowledge management platform. However, the rating will be subjective so in the end it would be great to have a discussion and ensure you have the same definitions.

1. **Criticality**

   Is this business-critical or a major opportunity?

   If ignored, would it materially harm the business or create a missed strategic opportunity?

   If yes → continue

   If no → continue to incremental value

   If don't know → Deep Dive

   Not every high-impact trend requires a strategic decision. Some are simply background conditions we operate within, and some things are simply the price of entry.

   Here, No means:

   Yes, this affects our business – but it does not materially change our strategic position, priorities or choices.

   In other words:

   It has impact, but it does not create leverage.

2. **Incremental value**

   Will it bring substantial incremental value now or in the future?

   If yes → Option

   If no → Discard

   If don't know → Deep Dive.

3. **Strategic recognition**

   Is this explicitly recognized in our current strategy?

   Not 'we talk about it', but 'it is visible in priorities, narratives or plans'.

   If yes → check execution reality

   If no → Act.

4. **Execution reality**

   Is there an active initiative or named owner?

   This exposes the gap between strategic intent and execution

   If yes → Inform

   If no → Act.

The five possible outcomes

Each trend ends in one of the following words:

Act → Commit resources, ownership, execution.

Inform → Shape strategic choices and leadership decisions.

Option → Take low-regret, reversible actions to stay prepared.

Deep Dive → Reduce uncertainty before deciding.

Discard → Consciously deprioritize for now. We choose not to act or prepare, because doing so creates no advantage for us right now.

Discard is a conscious choice not to commit, not a denial.

If you are not ready to *Act*, but it feels risky to *Discard*, you should *Option*.

This is where the Lab becomes both de-risking and opportunity-opening.

Output

For each selected trend, you produce:

- A one-word decision posture.
- A shared understanding of why that posture was chosen.

This is not a list of initiatives. It is a governance tool that makes leadership intent visible.

What Your Decision Sets in Motion

Every posture carries consequences and comes with trade-offs.

Once you decide whether you will *Act, Inform, Option, Deep Dive* or *Discard*, you are shaping how risk accumulates in your organization over time. This changes attention, investment and energy.

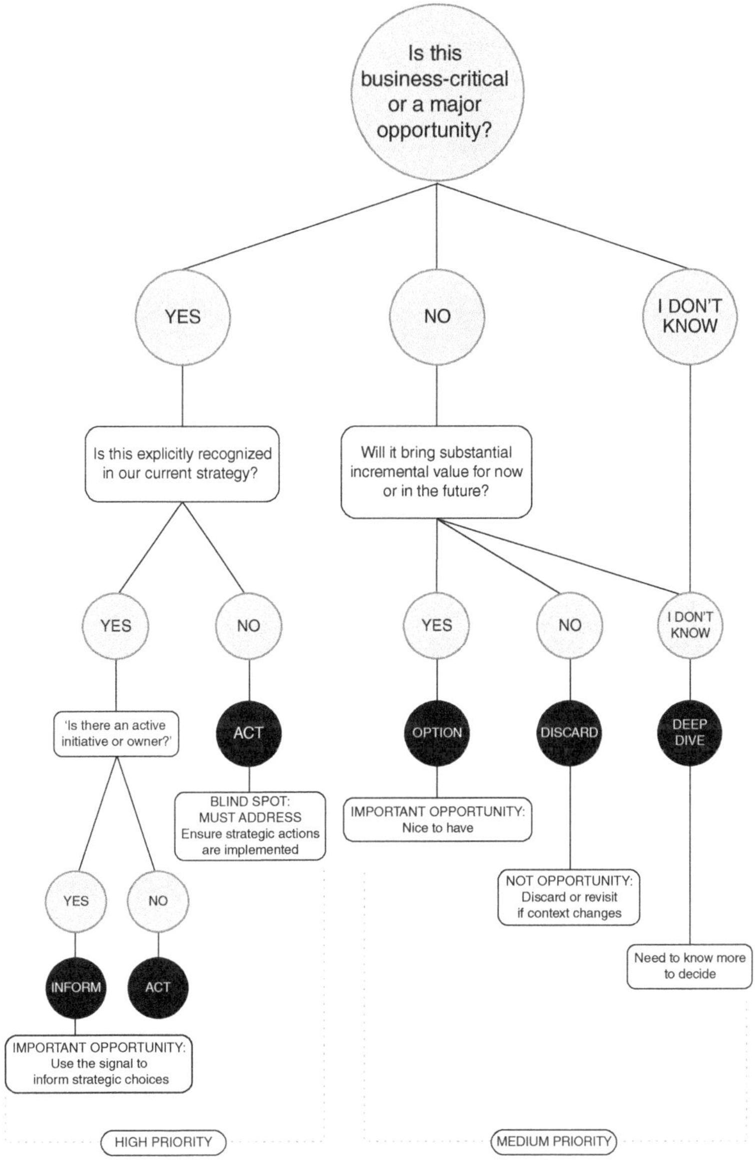

Figure 6.2 Strategic Decision Tree.

Let's now look at what each posture could set in motion.

Act

Short Term (0–12 Months) Momentum increases. There are clearly selected and named owners, budget is allocated, the organization feels and acts decisively and proactively. There is a sense of mobilization, motivation and pride. Executing begins. This means:

- Resources are visibly allocated.
- Internal alignment strengthens.
- Accountability becomes clearer.

Mid Term (1–3 Years) If the bet proves right, advantage compounds, but if the external forces evolve differently and no course correction is carried out then sunk-cost bias may start appearing. At this point:

- Investments deepen exposure.
- Capabilities scale.
- Strategic rigidity may increase.

Long Term (3–5+ Years) There are two options here: you either lead in this space decisively, or carry the burden of having overcommitted.

Act can build a strong current of strength, but only if the underlying signal persists.

Inform

Short Term (0–12 Months) The foresight shapes leadership thinking but does not yet trigger decisive structural moves. This means:

- Strategy language shifts.
- Decision-making becomes more aware.
- Capital remains largely unchanged.

Mid Term (1–3 Years) If the signal strengthens, *Inform* can convert into *Act*. It's important to have the right forums and cadence to review this category and force decision-making, because if ignored for too long, reaction may have to become urgent and not benefit from the luxury of being deliberate and strategic. As a result:

- Internal tension may grow.
- Other alternative options may appear and move faster.
- Narrative shifts precede operational shifts.

Long Term (3–5+ Years) *Inform* without progression risks becoming passive monitoring. If the trend becomes less or more relevant, probable or impactful, then it should enter one of the other spaces and the respective action should be taken.

Option

Short Term (0–12 Months) Small and reversible bets are placed. This looks like:

- Pilot initiatives.
- Capability experiments.
- Scenario testing.

Mid Term (1–3 Years) Optionality creates a level of flexibility. While you are not overexposed, you are also not leading either. As a result:

- Switching costs remain manageable.
- Learning accumulates.

Long Term (3–5+ Years) If exercised at the right time, *Option* becomes strategic acceleration, but if left standing idle, then it becomes merely symbolic and has no positive effect on the organization.

Deep Dive

Short Term (0–12 Months) Uncertainty is acknowledged rather than masked and new knowledge is being delivered, informing next steps and leading to choices. This presents as:

- Research commissioned.
- Expertise consulted.
- Assumptions clarified.

Mid Term (1–3 Years) Clarity emerges, but beware of prolonged analysis as it can delay necessary positioning and choice.

Long Term (3–5+ Years) If foresight is acted upon, resilience improves. If not, exposure increases.

Discard

Short Term (0–12 Months) Resources stay focused and simplicity increases.

Mid Term (1–3 Years) If the force truly remains peripheral, the decision and this discipline pays off. However, if it intensifies, you are already behind.

Long Term (3–5+ Years) *Discard* is powerful when it's a conscious decision, but can be very dangerous if impact is underestimated or the choice is made out of convenience.

Mini Example: Early AI Governance as Advantage

A mid-sized fintech company anticipated regulatory tightening around algorithmic bias before formal enforcement. Rather than waiting for legislation, they published voluntary transparency standards and implemented third-party auditing. This meant:

Short term: higher compliance costs.

Medium term: preferred vendor status with enterprise clients.

Long term: trust became a structural moat.

Responsibility created differentiation.

Company: global consumer electronics manufacturer
Time horizon: five years
Context: strong brand, premium positioning, global expansion

The executive team runs this Lab at an annual strategy forum. They begin with 18 identified trends across all STEEP categories.

After mapping on the Probability × Impact matrix, five land in the 'Strategically Important Now' zone:

1. AI regulation tightening globally.
2. Rising customer demand for repairability.
3. Growth of AI-generated synthetic reviews and content.
4. Youth-driven anti-consumption sentiment.
5. Geopolitical fragmentation affecting supply chains.

With those determined, it's time to put each of these through the Strategic Decision Tree. Here are two examples of how this might play out.

Trend: AI Regulation Tightening

Business Criticality? Yes, it impacts product roadmap and compliance.
Strategic recognition? Not explicitly embedded.
Execution reality? No owner.

→ Decision posture: Act

Short Term (0–12 months)

- Legal + Product taskforce formed.
- Compliance roadmap initiated.
- AI governance policy published.

Mid Term (1–3 years)

- First-mover advantage in trust positioning.
- Higher development cost but stronger credibility.

Long Term (3–5+ years)

- Regulatory trust becomes a competitive moat.

Trend: Youth Anti-Consumption

Business Criticality? Uncertain.
Strategic recognition? Discussed but not embedded.

(continued)

(*continued*)

→ **Decision posture: Option**

Short Term (0–12 months)

- Small experiment in modular repairable devices.

Mid Term (1–3 years)

- Signals monitored (policy shifts, social campaigns, resale market growth).

Long Term (3–5+ years)

- If sentiment scales → pivot product design philosophy.

What an efficient and productive meeting. The team now leaves the workshop with five clearly owned decisions and a roadmap, not with 18 pieces of information to worry about!

The CEO can now talk confidently in front of the board to articulate the strategy, which external shifts will impact us most and show which we are already acting on. They can also outline which ones we are monitoring and preparing for, and highlight the ones we are aware of, but consciously not prioritizing (for now, unless they become more probable and impactful).

What's Your Move?

Now that you've filtered the noise, forced perspective-sharing and turned 'outside forces' into decision logic, we come to the part CEOs care about. The question you are ready to answer is:

Which risks and opportunities are we actively responding to — and which are we choosing not to manage yet?

Because you are always choosing, whether you do it with intent or not.

How This Connects to the Futures Strategy Canvas

The output of this Lab feeds directly into the external forces and decision posture sections of the Canvas (see Figure 6.3).

The trends you *Act* on define exposure.

The ones you *Discard* define risk tolerance.

The ones you *Option* define optionality.

This is how responsibility becomes embedded in governance rather than just rhetoric.

What Goes into the Futures Strategy Canvas

Write down:

1. Your 'Strategically Important Now' List
   A short list (ideally 5–10) of the external risks/opportunities you selected.
2. Grouped by the decision posture
   ACT, INFORM, OPTION, DEEP DIVE, DISCARD

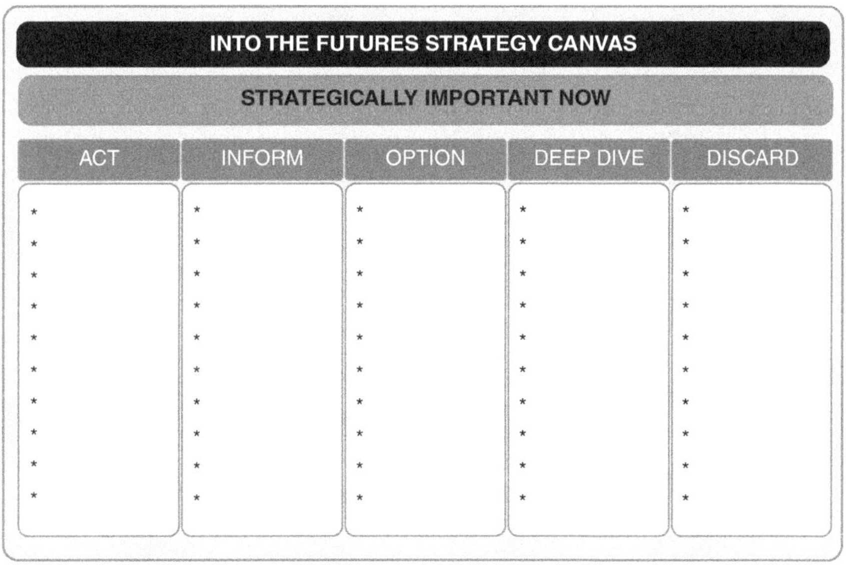

Figure 6.3 What You Carry Forward: Into the Futures Strategy Canvas.

Optional Reflection

Which trend did we disagree most on and why?

Which 'opportunity' felt uncomfortable because it requires change?

Where are we most tempted to delay because we lack certainty?

Head to www.futures-forward.com to download the tool templates.

Ready for the next Lab?

Continue Your Strategic Path

This Lab focused on trends, which are most likely to impact your business, and how you can move forwards with this foresight.

If your next question is about who your customer of the future might be, move to **Strategic Futures Lab 1**.

If uncertainty sits around whether your product will be relevant in the future, work through **Strategic Futures Lab 2**.

If the tension you feel relates to innovation, continue to **Strategic Futures Lab 4**.

If you want to know whether your current strategy will remain resilient in the future, go to **Strategic Futures Lab 5.**

Remember, each Lab stands alone and they don't have to be completed in any particular order.

This is meant to be a choose-your-own-path playbook and you should follow the tension that feels most relevant for your organization.

7 Strategic Futures Lab 4: Where Are the Best Opportunities for Innovation?

Tool: Future Opportunity Mapping

Innovation capacity is finite, and where you choose to spend it shapes what your company becomes. This Strategic Futures Lab is about these deliberate, consciously made choices.

Meet Your Future Self — Your POV

You are the Vice President of Growth and Innovation at a great company. The brand is well-respected, selling quality products and through time, it has avoided dramatic shocks and pivots. At a first glance, there is no need to worry. On a second glance, you are looking at some worrying signals that hint to an even greater need for innovation.

Growth has not collapsed but it has flattened. Keeping up with the results year on year seems to require more and more effort. There isn't a lack of new ideas, the company is open to employee engagement and generally the culture is trustworthy and teams are passionate about the product and the brand. Unfortunately, very few of these new ideas survive the journey from idea presentation to commitment. The reason for that is not the quality of the ideas but a problem that must be faced: the level of certainty the organization expects, and therefore the risk it's willing to take.

In a recent executive session, the CEO summed it up in a couple of sentences:

'We are not looking for big uncertain bets. We are a small company and can't afford big risks. We should be looking at focused, realistic innovation'.

Everyone around the table silently agreed with the CEO, or at least no one objected. However, as the conversation continued you kept observing the same pattern. Anything that felt new was reframed as premature, too risky or out of scope. The leadership team found various reasons to reject an idea. The only ideas that remained were those that fitted all too well into existing capabilities, timelines and metrics.

You left the meeting asking yourself whether the definition of innovation has the same meaning to you as to the rest of the team. You carried the uneasy feeling that you might be slowly designing yourselves out of relevance, opening up the opportunity for cannibalization and covering this fear of risk with the stance that you're being disciplined.

You left the meeting with a question you've been carrying for a while now:

> *If innovation capacity is finite, why are we spending it only on extensions of the past?*

What bothers you most is not the rejection of ideas, but the behavioural pattern behind it.

You started to notice that every proposal that stretches beyond today's capabilities is labelled as irresponsible and not viable, topic closed. The language used in the room sounds rational: 'We need evidence', 'The market is not ready', 'Let's focus on what we know works …' and none of this is technically wrong. But that doesn't make it right either. It makes it complacent and dangerous.

This company is not allergic to innovation, but it seems to be allergic to ambiguity. Ironically, ambiguity is exactly the condition under which innovation has to happen!

You realize that the organization has conditioned itself to become very good at refining existing categories, improving the packaging here and there, slowly expanding distribution and adding safe, common sense features to products. But for some reason, there are not enough conversations about the real problems people care about and whether these are shifting in response to a changing living and operating environment.

One thing you are certain about is that you are not trying to turn the company into a reckless venture lab, although you might be accused of that sometimes. And what you can see, but others struggle to, is that it seems that discipline and caution have slowly turned into self-limitation.

That is the exact tension this Lab exists to address.

In the last few months you have started hearing the same faint message from a variety of places, delivered in different shapes and forms. These messages are starting to build a pattern, a fuller picture. Customers seem to be asking more for reassurance and not so much about product features. A partner hints that a new distribution channel is opening but brands that can meet stricter requirements for transparency (even though the legislation does not yet require that) will be given the priority to run pilots. The recruiters are coming back with feedback from candidates saying they would love to be at the forefront of innovation. These candidates see an opportunity to radically change the business, partially because they haven't seen a real innovation come out of the pipeline, despite having such a high opinion of the brand.

You are seeing **a window**, an opportunity to act and to take this organization into the future. It's one of those moments when the environment is showing you the opportunity, the brand has the foundations and the organization has the resource. The only thing that needs to change is the tolerance to uncertainty and understanding how to manage innovation to succeed.

You decide to bring this up to the leadership meeting as a careful conversation and a very strategic and measured approach. You say something like: 'There's an opening here, an opportunity, and it's not just for a random innovation project. This opportunity opens up for a deliberate exploration into where a lot of value lies dormant and we have the assets to unlock it first'.

The familiar organizational reflex shows up, but the CEO asks you to make your case. You know that this journey will take time and involve change management, but this is what you came here to do. The CEO promises to champion the idea if he is convinced. There are resources he is willing to deploy for a 'carefully managed' exploration. You spearhead this expedition into the future, because, in your role, you are not paid to protect comfort. You are paid to protect future advantage.

This Lab is a way to stop arguing about whether innovation should be bold or cautious, the answer is not black or white. Instead you can make a more useful decision: where, specifically, **exploration is justified, and where it is not**.

The Leadership Question

Where should we deliberately innovate and where should we choose not to?

And I want to point out here that this question is not one for creativity. It is a selectivity question.

Why This Lab Exists

Generally, irrespective of whether a company is large or small, leadership teams should agree on three things:

- The future will not look like the present.
- Not everything deserves investment.
- Innovation capacity is finite.

What they also have to agree on is:

- Where innovation is justified.
- Why those areas matter.
- What uncertainty they are willing to engage with.

Most organizations talk about innovation as if it starts with ideas. In reality, innovation is constrained much earlier by what leaders choose to pay attention to, explore and legitimize under uncertainty.

This Lab exists to force a choice about where exploration is warranted before ideas, roadmaps or funding debates begin.

How This Lab Works

You will:

1. Identify stressed human needs.
2. Translate them into structural tensions.
3. Define opportunity spaces.
4. Filter at leadership level.
5. Select only two to three justified domains.
6. Assign them to innovation horizons.

This is a discipline of selection, not idea generation.

What This Lab Is (and Is Not)

This Lab is:

- A way to define future-facing opportunity spaces.
- A method to prioritize exploration domains.
- A leadership decision about attention and learning.

This Lab is not:

- An idea brainstorming session.
- A portfolio allocation exercise.
- A commitment to build anything.

Inputs

You can run this Lab in two ways.

If you have completed earlier Labs, you can bring forward:

- Future relevance arenas (Lab 1).
- Product relevance decisions (Lab 2).
- Decision posture themes (Lab 3).

If not, use the baseline future pressure that follows.

Baseline Future Pressure

Assume a future environment where:

- Trust is harder to earn and easier to lose.
- Automation increasingly mediates decision-making.
- Efficiency and resilience are both expected.
- Legitimacy and transparency shape adoption.

We are not looking at this as a forecast. We use this information as a baseline decision environment.

The Tool: Future Opportunity Mapping

Future Opportunity Mapping is an original decision tool introduced in this book.

Its purpose is to:

- Translate future pressure into human tension.
- Convert tension into opportunity spaces.
- Force leadership-level selection.

It produces opportunity intent, but does not focus on solutions.

Step 1 — Select Stressed Human Needs

From the list below, select no more than three human needs that feel most strained under the future conditions described above (see Figure 7.1):

- Safety & security
- Control & autonomy
- Trust & fairness
- Belonging & identity
- Competence & confidence
- Meaning & purpose
- Convenience & efficiency

Don't attempt to select all relevant needs. Instead, only choose the ones that are experiencing the greatest future strain. We are looking to work within constraint, which reveals true priority.

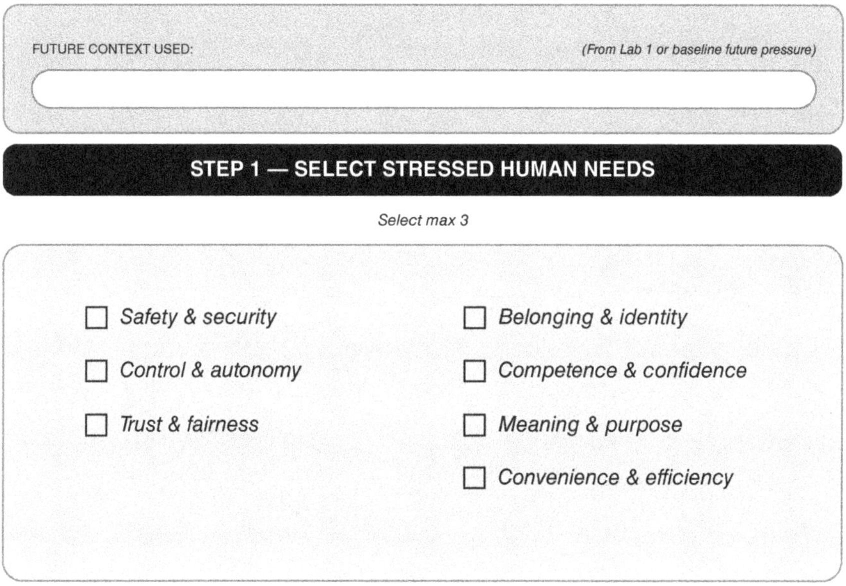

Figure 7.1 Future Opportunity Mapping. Step 1.

Step 2 — Articulate the Core Tensions

For each selected need, complete the sentence:

> ***People increasingly need [enter the need], but the future makes this harder because [constraint or pressure].***

For example: people increasingly need **trust,** but **automation reduces visibility** and **accountability** (see Figure 7.2).

Think of tensions not as temporary problems, but structural frictions that appear when systems, expectations and values shift. They cannot be solved immediately, but will require solutions in the future.

STEP 2 — ARTICULATE THE CORE TENSIONS

For each selected need, complete the sentence:

NEED 01: __________

People increasingly need__________________ but the future makes this harder because__________________.

NEED 02: __________

People increasingly need__________________ but the future makes this harder because__________________.

NEED 03: __________

People increasingly need__________________ but the future makes this harder because__________________.

Figure 7.2 Future Opportunity Mapping. Step 2.

Step 3 — Define Opportunity Spaces (Not Ideas)

Convert each tension into an opportunity space.

Opportunity Space

> ***Supporting [actor] to [resolve the tension] in a world where [future condition applies].***

For example: supporting **non-expert users** to **feel capable and informed** in a world where **complexity is hidden behind intelligent systems** (see Figure 7.3).

Rules

Stay abstract at this stage, keep the spaces open enough that you aren't determining a course of action. That means no products or features.

If it reads like a solution, it isn't an opportunity space.

A strong opportunity space should still make sense in 5–10 years, even if today's technologies or business models change.

Teams should generate 4–6 opportunity spaces at this stage.

Only once opportunity spaces are defined do leadership decisions begin.

STEP 3 — DEFINE OPPORTUNITY SPACES (NOT IDEAS)

Supporting [actor] to [resolve tension] when [condition]

OPPORTUNITY SPACE 01:

Supporting ____________________ ***to*** ____________________

in a world where ____________________ .

OPPORTUNITY SPACE 02:

Supporting ____________________ ***to*** ____________________

in a world where ____________________ .

OPPORTUNITY SPACE 03:

Supporting ____________________ ***to*** ____________________

in a world where ____________________ .

OPPORTUNITY SPACE 04:

Supporting ____________________ ***to*** ____________________

in a world where ____________________ .

OPPORTUNITY SPACE 05:

Supporting ____________________ ***to*** ____________________

in a world where ____________________ .

OPPORTUNITY SPACE 06:

Supporting ____________________ ***to*** ____________________

in a world where ____________________ .

Figure 7.3 Future Opportunity Mapping. Step 3.

Step 4 — Leadership Opportunity Filter

Each opportunity space is tested against four questions (see Figure 7.4):

1. **Human pain:** is the tension costly, risky or emotionally loaded?
2. **Future persistence:** does it matter across multiple plausible futures?
3. **Brand right to play:** does our brand or company have legitimacy, assets or capability here? Or would it make sense to build them in the future?
4. **Value logic:** would someone plausibly pay, commit or change behaviour?

Rule: only opportunity spaces that pass at least three of four proceed. It's important to make conscious choices about your brand. Something may

Figure 7.4 Future Opportunity Mapping. Step 4.

not have a commercial uptake, but may have a positive impact on your brand perception. I would not advise you to take on opportunities that do the opposite — by which I mean are commercially attractive but are misaligned with your brand.

It's important here to bring in the leadership experience and honest evaluation of the assets of the brand that are not easy to imitate.

A great example of Right to Play is Nike launching Nike Run Club. Anyone could have created a running app, but the authentic credibility of Nike lies in the ecosystem – product integration, behavioural data, long-standing trust. It is not the actual application that presents the opportunity, but rather the encouragement and the performance in a digitally-based fitness environment that is more difficult to replicate without the backing of the Nike brand and its associated cultural influence.

Before we move onto the final steps in this tool, let's look at how these first four steps can lead to a shift in mindset that has the power to transform an organization.

Company: mid-sized consumer health and lifestyle brand
Time Horizon: 1–3 years
Context: recently lost a market opportunity due to internal hesitation.

The company recently declined a partnership proposal from a digital health platform that was rapidly expanding. This happened three months ago and the decision was taken quickly. The opportunity concerned the next two cycles, it wasn't focused on the distant future. It was specific, near-term and operational.

This proposal required a well-coordinated process across various teams: product development, brand, planning, commercial, legal. It was implementable had they decided to move forward with it.

Sadly, the organization hesitated and missed the opportunity. Part of the decision was procedural. The board needed more evidence and the potential partner seemed a little too ambitious, a little too aggressive and quick. This worried the leadership team who felt that the style and bias toward action may lead to brand health damage.

(*continued*)

(continued)

All of these were reasonable concerns, of course, and based on rational thinking. But when the decision was reviewed in hindsight, weeks later when it was evident the opportunity was there and it was missed: what became clear was that it wasn't the lack of information that failed them, it was the accepted tolerance and lack of process for engaging with uncertainty.

When the process lacks, when there is no tolerance or agreed threshold, every opportunity that comes the business's way and carries ambiguity would always be met with a default answer: no. And that is not because caution is the right strategic approach in every single of these cases. It is because the framework to distinguish between reckless exposure and disciplined exploration is simply missing.

And that recognition led to the decision to run Lab 4.

This is a deliberate attempt to clarify where, in the next 1–3 years, ambiguity will be justified.

Step 1 — Selecting the Needs Under Strain

Anchoring the time horizon in 1–3 years changes the discussion from total uncertainty to a clearer indication where the future needs of customers lie. The outlook in this horizon is more realistically projected and after individual reflections and group discussions, the leadership team identified the top three needs under pressure:

1. Control & autonomy
2. Competence & confidence
3. Meaning & purpose

The missed partnership had touched all three.

1. Control: over how and where the brand appeared.
2. Competence: in evaluating new operating models.
3. Meaning: in protecting coherence while evolving.

Step 2 — Articulating the Core Tensions

Once they were named, the tensions became a lot clearer than when the original partnership debate was happening.

Customers already expect increasingly integrated well-being experiences. But the brand was structured around isolated offerings.

Customers expect guidance and convincing storytelling that goes alongside the products they sell. Yet this experience was not possible without collaboration beyond the traditionally established boundaries by the company.

Even though the brand wanted to preserve image and coherence, it allowed this to become rigidity.

So the conversation shifted from: 'Why didn't we make the right call?' to 'What operating logic are we prepared to build for the next three years?'

Step 3 — Defining the Opportunity Spaces

Based on the tensions, the team was able to outline a few opportunity spaces. These are not products or campaigns but arenas that their company would be willing to explore.

- Supporting guided well-being journeys beyond standalone products.
- Building repeatable collaboration frameworks for selective ecosystem partnerships.
- Strengthening internal capability for structured pilots without full strategic exposure.
- Developing brand governance tools that enable evolution without dilution.

What is interesting is how the conversation elevates from debating SKUs to discussing the decision-making architecture that allows for future growth and expansion.

(*continued*)

(continued)

Step 4 — Applying the Leadership Filter

In this particular example, when the four criteria were applied – human relevance, future persistence within the 1–3 years horizon, right to play and value logic – two opportunity spaces stood out as both strategically coherent and operationally plausible:

1. Building a repeatable pilot-partnership framework.
2. Extending product lines into structured guidance programs.

These felt aligned and made sense. For the first time since the missed opportunity, the organization had language for selection vs justification.

The CEO's reflection sums this up perfectly:

'The decision to decline that partnership may or may not have been correct. What wasn't correct was that we didn't know what kind of uncertainty we are built to engage with'.

This Lab doesn't just help in one situation. It also ensures the right mindset and process is in place for when the next opportunity comes along.

Distinguishing Incremental vs Transformative

As part of the leadership opportunity filter, you also need to decide whether the innovation you are exploring is incremental or transformative. Here's where the difference between the two lies:

Incremental innovation improves existing offerings within today's value logic.

Transformative innovation questions the value logic itself.

A useful test:

- If the opportunity space strengthens your current business model → incremental.
- If it reshapes how value is created, captured or distributed → transformative.

Both are legitimate, the key is explicit selection.

A Practical Allocation Discipline: 70/20/10

Finding the right balance between exploiting existing ideas and resources, and exploring for innovation is individual and specific to each organization. But a good starting point when it comes to how much innovation should be happening in each horizon is the 70/20/10 rule. This is fully flexible, according to your ambition and risk tolerance.

The classification across Horizon 1, Horizon 2 and Horizon 3 loosely follows the Three Horizons framework developed at McKinsey, which helps organizations balance strengthening today's business while exploring emerging opportunities.[1]

To ensure exploration does not either overwhelm or disappear, many organizations apply a simple allocation discipline across horizons:

- 70% of innovation effort in Horizon 1.
- 20% in Horizon 2.
- 10% in Horizon 3.

The 70% ensures that the existing business model continues to generate the strength that funds future exploration. **Horizon 1 protects continuity**.

The 20% in **Horizon 2 protects adaptability**. It builds the organization's ability to pilot, partner and learn without destabilizing operations.

The 10% in **Horizon 3 protects optionality**. It allows the company to explore structural shifts deliberately rather than reactively.

In a 1–3 years strategic cycle, this distribution reassures stakeholders that ambition is bounded. It makes exposure visible instead of accidental.

Without an explicit declaration of what the distribution will look like, Horizon 1 will almost always consume the majority of the attention. By explicitly announcing the intended distribution across all three horizons, you make your innovation posture intentional.

Step 5 — Classify Uncertainty

Before making the final selection, apply a light classification to each opportunity space to clarify the level of uncertainty involved (see Figure 7.5).

Time Horizon

- Near term (1–2 years)
- Mid term (3–5 years)
- Long term (5+ years)

This step defines the learning requirements and governance.

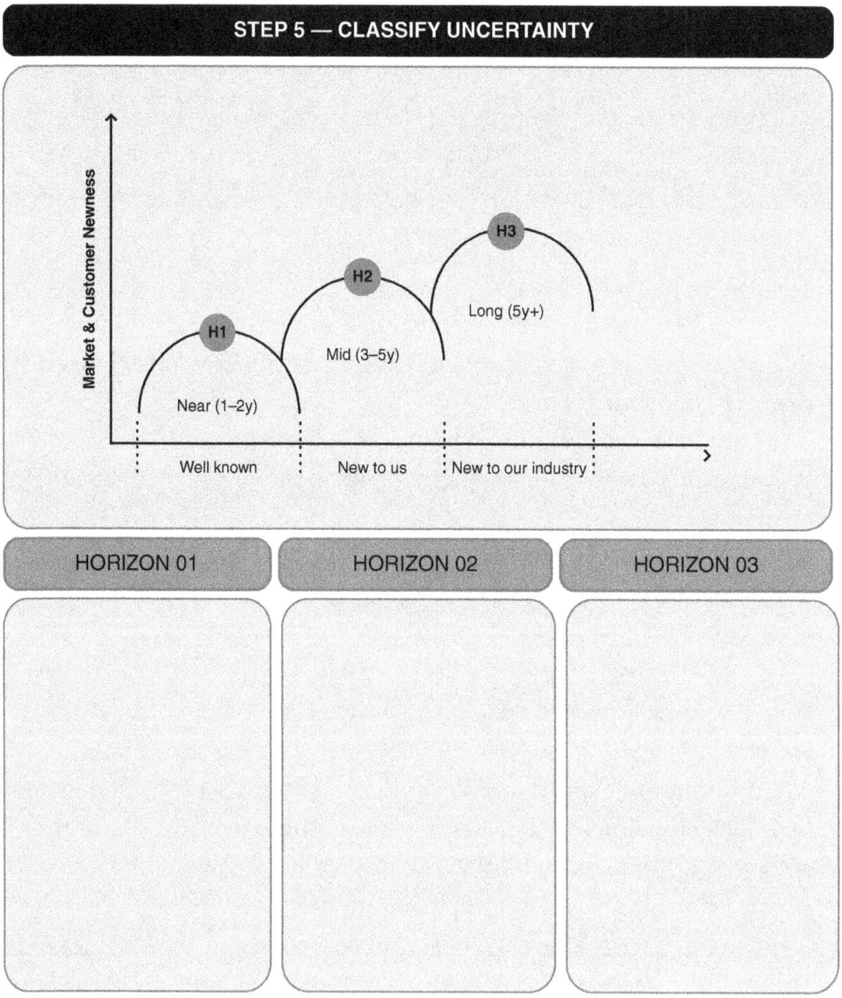

Figure 7.5 Future Opportunity Mapping. Step 5.

Step 6 — Select Where Innovation Is Justified

Leaders select **2–3 opportunity spaces** where exploration is justified and explicitly deprioritize the rest (see Figure 7.6).

Choosing means:

- Allowing experimentation.
- Allocating attention.
- Accepting uncertainty.

Everything else is explicitly deprioritized.

Not now does not mean not ever. There are many spaces in literature that speak about running innovation teams and the benefit of keeping a log of ideas, even failed ideas! There is a huge amount of learning that the innovation process can provide, whether an idea comes to life or not.

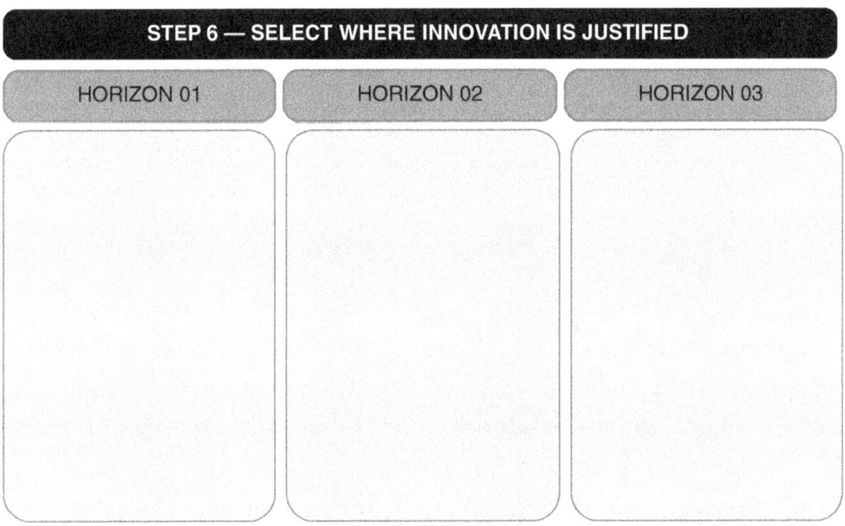

Figure 7.6 Future Opportunity Mapping. Step 6.

What Your Innovation Posture Sets in Motion

Selecting opportunity spaces and assigning them to horizons is an important step as it reshapes behaviour over time, but it is also extremely rewarding. You are able to organize the chaos of uncertainty and turn it into opportunities that start to live in logical compartments, each able to be addressed by its own set of actions.

Let's look at the possible consequences of taking this approach.

If Innovation Remains Concentrated in Horizon 1

Short Term (0–12 Months) Execution is relatively smooth, the investment debates are not too complicated because resources remain aligned with the current operating model. Change is not too drastic and it feels safe. It's met with low resistance.

Mid Term (1–3 Years) The organization becomes increasingly proficient at optimization, but less practiced at experimentation. Partnership conversations or adjacent models continue to feel structurally uncomfortable.

Long Term (3–5+ Years) When structural shifts require movement, the transition feels abrupt rather than evolutionary. Capability gaps must be closed quickly instead of gradually.

In short, stability is maintained, but optionality narrows.

If a Balanced Distribution Is Applied (Approx. 70/20/10)

Short Term (0–12 Months) Some friction appears as Horizon 2 initiatives require protection from short-term financial scrutiny. Governance becomes clearer.

Mid Term (1–3 Years) Pilot structures become repeatable. Ambiguous opportunities are evaluated through staged logic rather than instinctive hesitation. The organization gains fluency in structured experimentation.

Long Term (3–5+ Years) As Horizon 2 initiatives mature, they transition into core capabilities. Horizon 3 explorations either integrate or are consciously closed, strengthening strategic discipline.

This means exposure remains measured and cumulative.

If Horizon 2 and 3 Expand Aggressively

Short Term (0–12 Months) Resource tension increases. Execution complexity grows. Leadership attention must stretch.

Mid Term (1–3 Years) If well-managed, adaptability becomes a visible competitive signal. If poorly managed, confusion around priorities increases.

Long Term (3–5+ Years) The organization may either emerge structurally stronger or overextended, depending entirely on governance discipline.

The takeaway is that ambition amplifies both upside and execution risk.

The consequence of this Lab is clarity. Not specifically about which idea to pursue, but about how to structure and compartmentalize uncertainty in a deliberate and controlled way.

By looking at innovations through the lens of the three horizons, we can also observe that ideas higher in novelty will likely belong to Horizon 2 or Horizon 3, versus Horizon 1.

How This Feeds the Futures Strategy Canvas

The opportunity spaces selected here become the innovation domains in the Canvas.

Horizon classification informs capability planning.

Explicit exclusions clarify trade-offs.

Without this Lab, the innovation section of the Canvas defaults to incrementalism.

What This Lab Produces

By the end of this Lab, leaders can say: these are the future opportunity spaces where innovation is justified – and these are the ones we are choosing not to pursue. A good strategy should identify the trade-offs, not focus on everyone and everything.

What Goes into the Futures Strategy Canvas

From Lab 4, the Canvas captures (see Figure 7.7):

- Selected opportunity spaces.
- Their linked human needs.
- Horizon and novelty tags.
- Explicit exclusions.

How ambidexterity plays out happens at the Canvas level, not here.

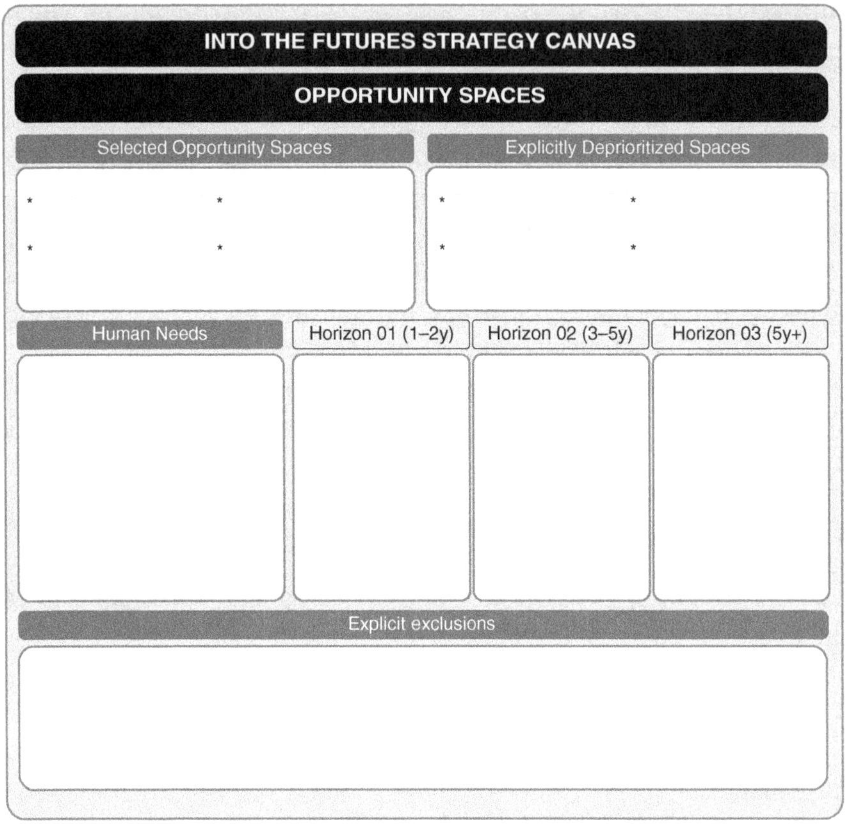

Figure 7.7 What You Carry Forward: Into the Futures Strategy Canvas.

Continue Your Strategic Path

This Lab focused on innovation opportunities, identifying opportunity spaces and determining how to balance innovation with continuity of business operations.

If your next question is about who your customer of the future might be, move to **Strategic Futures Lab 1**.

If uncertainty sits around whether your product will be relevant in the future, look at **Strategic Futures Lab 2**.

If the tension you feel relates to future opportunities and risks you must address today, go to **Strategic Futures Lab 3**.

If you want to know whether your current strategy will remain resilient in the future, continue to **Strategic Futures Lab 5.**

Each Lab stands alone and they don't have to be completed in any particular order.

This is meant to be a choose-your-own-path playbook and you should follow the tension that feels most relevant for your organization.

8 Strategic Futures Lab 5: Will My Strategy Still Work in the Future?

Tool: Strategic Wind Tunneling Toolkit

Welcome to your Strategic Futures Lab 5. Here, you're not just going to read about the future; you will learn how to test the resilience of your strategy against it!

Meet Your Future Self — Your POV

You are the Chief Strategy Officer (CSO) of Xterion Corp and even though you usually start your Mondays early, today you've already had your third coffee before 8 am. This week the tension is building up, you can cut it with a knife. The board meeting is in six weeks and you are feeling, to put it mildly, uneasy.

You have doubts that are keeping you up at night. The five-year Corporate Strategy and Financial Plan will be presented for final sign off. This strategy has been the company's darling and something the C-Suite worked very hard to develop. It is consistent with the strategy from the previous planning cycle, which delivered double-digit growth, stable brand positioning and made shareholders happy. It also bagged you that promotion to a CSO! You are beginning to realize that sometimes it's easier to get to the top than remain there.

You stare at the pile of reports on your desk. All of them are screaming that something is shifting and making you question the resilience of the choices made. Your gut feeling says this isn't the right approach. The plans were built based on historical information and a very different operating environment.

The new customer research report from last quarter arrived yesterday and evoked slight panic. The agency is sharing subtle signals of change, but overlaying them with your experience, the looming macro uncertainty and the insights from the research, you are no longer certain the strategy will hold. A hard dilemma stands in front of you. You can't predict the future and you can't upset the C-Suite. You all have to come united in front of the board and you had better have a great justification as to any changes you propose to the strategy. How do you do that when there is no quantifiable evidence? Yet, how can you ever have evidence for something set in the future? You can back up the existing strategy plan that you no longer believe in, or you can find a way to substantiate your hypothesis and make changes that will help the strategy become more resilient and relevant to the future.

You can't ignore some of the nagging questions:

- Will this strategy still be relevant in five years?
- Will the new generation resonate with the brand?
- How do we ensure resilience if the turmoil we are sensing comes true?

It's not your first rodeo, you have been at a similar place before. Market ups and downs, new generations, new needs, choices and values, unexpected competitor moves. However, this time the narrative around the shifts speaks of something far more substantial. It almost feels like watching storm clouds gather, while everyone is enjoying a nice summer day at the beach. You have to make sure you are well-prepared to answer the tough questions your CEO will undoubtedly ask.

Let's look at everything we know...

Current Strategy

Your original strategy was built on three pillars that made complete sense two years ago when the C-Suite began crafting it. It was based on market dynamics, undeniable past success and a set of underlying assumptions that were deemed low-risk at that time.

- Pillar 1: premium positioning in established on- and offline retail channels, because that's where the money came from.
- Pillar 2: product innovation through small iterations and minimal improvements, because customers loved every 2.0 version so far.
- Pillar 3: geographical expansion into emerging markets, because continuous growth has to come from somewhere.

Let's take a closer look at why these pillars seemed like a solid foundation to the strategy and what the assumptions were.

Pillar 1: Premium Positioning in Established On- and Offline Retail Channels Why it made sense:

- The retail partners had existing infrastructure that allowed for the fastest expansion and that's where the money was flowing from.
- Customers trusted the retail brands and there was a legacy of reliable collaboration.
- Premium price was perceived as a sign of premium quality and brand credibility.

Core assumptions:

- Economy, spending power and retail formats remain relatively stable.
- Retail partners will continue to prioritize brand-led partnerships, maintain premium shelfspace and support loyal collaborators like Xterion Corp.
- Premium positioning will continue to mean high quality, relevance and desirability, which means profit.

Pillar 2: Product Innovation Through Small Iterations and Minimal Improvements, Because Customers Loved Every 2.0 Version So Far
Core assumptions:

- Product satisfied customers' functional needs and that will continue to be enough.
- Incremental innovation is sufficient to remain relevant.
- Everything works so well, why make any changes?

Pillar 3: Geographical Expansion into Emerging Markets, Because Continuous Growth Has to Come from Somewhere
Core assumptions:

- Our universal product is surely globally transferable and our model can be replicated across new markets with only slight modifications.
- Global supply chains will remain resilient and cost-efficient.
- Legal and geopolitical environments in the priority emerging markets will remain permissive and business-friendly.

Now that we have explored the assumptions based on which the strategy was built, let's take a look at the uncomfortable and alarming truths that the reports are showing.

The Emerging Signals of Change

Signal 1: The Emerging Conscious Unconsumer The customer research revealed something unusual. Gen Alpha focus groups kept mentioning words like 'authentic', 'impact' and 'activism' when discussing brands they love. When asked about your flagship products, one respondent said, 'They're okay, I guess. But I try to be a "conscious unconsumer" (a term coined by the author), so I wonder if I really need them. What are they really for? The brand doesn't vibe, the products don't increase my dopamine, they don't trigger a positive emotional response! So why should I buy them?' This isn't the brand loyalty assumption you built your career on. How do you respond to something like that?

In addition to that, customers are measuring how you are treating your employees, suppliers, the community and the planet. They are looking at whether that matches what your social media communicates.

This research doesn't show a rejection of your brand per se. It shows something bigger than that and deserves you to sit with this tension. It's a shift in the reasons and assumptions as to why people consume.

Signal 2: Customer Agency Through Co-creation and Personalization Beyond the need for the products and brands to resonate with the cultural and value system of the audience, there is another shift that can easily disrupt the business model. Today's customers expect to be collaborators, to have their voice heard, to see their ideas and identities represented in the products, to have their creativity acknowledged. The tools are already available. One of the enablers is the accessibility of AI. Other industry players are already experimenting, fast. You have debated this, but your company wants to make sure you move transparently and ethically and with the best interest of the customer in mind. As a result, it is reluctant to make risky moves while there is no appropriate regulation.

The Head of Key Accounts, who just returned from a partner meeting, is feeling concerned. 'Everyone's talking about co-creation', she told you. 'Soon it won't just be a side hustle anymore. It will be the main event. With our operating model, how do we plan on addressing this need? Do we know what customers will want in five years' time? Everything changes so fast, we can't keep up'.

However, this caution is viewed as inertia by some of your partners. Your number one retail partner sent a barely concealed threat about shelf space if you don't change your approach to shifting customer expectations.

Signal 3: The Retail Landscape is Shifting Your top retail partner is reallocating the premium shelf space you are currently occupying to brands with adaptive models. In other words, those who personalize experiences and respond to customers' needs and wants swiftly. They are not cutting you out yet, but this looks more and more like a possibility you would have never imagined, considering your long-standing relationship with them.

Signal 4: Macro Factors are Already Impacting the Operations of the Business Then the Operations Director called. The supply chain disruptions that you all thought were temporary? He just reported that they are here to stay. Companies are facing tougher requirements for extensive checks on environmental and social impacts in their supply chains, and your current global model is looking unsustainably costly and risky.

Indonesia, poised to become the world's number four economy by 2030, naturally is one of the emerging markets that your strategy focuses on. It represents 35% of your projected incremental growth. But cultural movement to protect local origins has erupted and #BanggaAsli is all over social media calling for a boycott of all Western brands that have local alternatives.

Signal 5: Legislation Moves Fast in Some Fields and Very Slow in Others Law on local sourcing passed in Indonesia as a response to the civil movement and this is an outcome you were not prepared for.

Meanwhile, AI legislation that isn't there yet is creating ambiguity, making decisions really hard to make.

Your legal team is 'monitoring developments', but the lack of proper regulation in AI is posing risks to your customers and prevents you from fully embracing it.

Your CEO wants answers and she has asked you to reassure the board your strategy is ready for the future. Not just 'it will work', but 'it will still matter to customers, it is resilient!'

What unsettles you most is not the exercise itself, but the possibility that the result may force a level of brutal honesty that will require dramatic changes.

So far, the strategy has lived as a coherent narrative. Everyone is supportive of it and it has worked okay to deliver results. It has been persuasive and has earned internal and external belief. Questioning it is not a simple and neutral act, because it touches reputations, past wins and political capital.

But what if more than one pillar weakens at once? What if the majority of actions feel incomplete and crumble under the pressure of the future worlds?

What if premium positioning begins to signal irrelevance rather than aspiration in certain markets? What if geographic expansion becomes entangled in political resistance faster than your teams can adapt? What if incremental product improvements feel disconnected from a generation that is questioning the premise of consumption altogether?

Wind tunneling is not designed to confirm that your strategy works. It is designed to reveal where it cracks, so you have to convince yourself that this exercise is not here to point fingers, but to illuminate what improvements are needed to succeed. None of the Labs have been introduced as simulations for comfort. All of them are rehearsals for consequences, such as:

- If the strategy breaks in two out of four futures, do you reinforce it?
- If it strains in every scenario but fails in none, is that resilience or fragility?
- If one pillar survives across all scenarios but two collapse repeatedly, do you have the courage to rebalance before performance forces the decision?

The real risk here is acting with confidence that isn't tested under the pressure of the future and cracks when you least expect it.

Time to put your strategy through the wind tunnel!

The Strategic Wind Tunneling Tools

This Lab uses a small set of tools that work together.

They are designed to be used in sequence and to answer one question only:

Is our current strategy resilient and if not, where does it break under future pressure?

You are not being asked to redesign your strategy here. You can take your existing strategies and simply test their relevance and resilience in four future worlds.

How the Tools Fit Together

- Future scenarios provide the pressure.
- The Wind Tunnel exposes weaknesses.
- The Resilience Gap Finder names where resilience fails.
- The Strategy Exposure Map reveals why.
- The Resilience Action Ladder helps you respond deliberately.
- Future Scenarios (Use as Inputs, Not Outputs).

Before testing your strategy, you need future conditions to test it against.

The four scenarios below are not forecasts and not teaching cases.

They exist purely to create pressure — to surface assumptions and vulnerabilities that remain invisible in a single expected future.

You can use the scenarios provided here, or replace them with scenarios developed internally or by a foresight partner.

There is no need to analyse the scenarios. Their only role is to reveal where your strategy works, strains or fails.

Future 1: The Unconsumption Revolution (2035)

By 2035 cultural relevance has taken the front stage, it's no longer just a marketing strategy. Brands are not only expected, but now forced, to take a stance and be vocal about who and what they support. The environmental damage has caused nearly 250 million people to migrate. There are several conflict zones, poverty and severe weather looming over humanity. Consumerism is now a term of the past. Every choice is automatically calculated and it comes off of a credit score, closely tied to the ethical, cultural and environmental footprint of each customer. Needless to say, the choices of the majority are focused on bare necessities, provided by brands that have a positive impact on the community and environment. What were traditional business models are no longer relevant. Continuous revenue growth targets are irrelevant and illegal. Legislation has enforced a 'People & Planet' score for each company selling services or products and monitors their scorecards closely. Customers aren't just shopping for a product, they want to buy a solution to a problem and a hopeful story that resonates with the set of values they carry. They want to know how your brand is improving the community and the environment.

Strategic Challenge

How does a brand stay emotionally and ethically relevant?

Future 2: The Agency Economy (2035)

AI has turned customers into the protagonists of their own stories. The default expectation is to be provided with options to customize and personalize your experience. Everyone seems to want to be a creator of their own destiny and brands are expected to engage customers in the innovation and execution process of their products. Customers design their own versions, be it packaging, features or ingredients, and they receive a profit share from it. Brands that collaborate with customers and turn them into business partners are thriving. But what's the trade-off? Huge complexity in operations and mindset. How can a brand that was built for legacy and consistency start acting like a flexible system? How does it differentiate from others? What does that brand's core identity become?

Strategic Challenge

How do you build a system that feels personal, responsive and scalable?

Future 3: In AI We Don't Trust (2035)

The digital landscape became filled with synthetic data and media. Fake news, fake product reviews, fake personalities that never existed are influencing millions of people. This has led to customers in 2035 being extremely sceptical not only of marketing, but anything that looks too good to be true. The AI fatigue has entered the lives of everyone. AI Free has been on the rise for the past 10 years and has become a huge selling point. Professions from the past have regained popularity. Everything that can show imperfection, human touch and craftsmanship is highly valued, over anything that comes from the mass market or is AI perfected. New forms of deliberate mistakes are coded into AI, but the scrutiny has reached the highest levels – people demand traceability to the human who worked on the product. Trust becomes the rarest currency and human traceability is required to prove the authenticity of a message, idea or product. In this world, efficiency is regarded with disdain. Being authentic, hard to fake and human is the sought-after premium.

Strategic Challenge

Where trust is proven through craft, and automation causes doubts, how can your brand remain profitable and credible?

Future 4: The Algorithm Knows Best (2035)

Life has become highly efficient. Everything is done on time and in the correct ratio, because the majority of tasks are automated. AI agents take most of the decisions. They manage purchases, agendas, people's health, what content they consume and who they need to speak to for optimal emotional satisfaction. Decisions happen in the shadows. They are optimized for convenience and the element of ad hoc discovery is minimized to nearly zero. Brand loyalty is no longer earned. It's paid for and embedded into the AI systems. The competition isn't for people's attention or retail shelf space, it's for algorithmic preference in the AI ecosystem, where the person using the product is absent from the choice-making process altogether.

Strategic Challenge

If AI curates every customer experience and chooses products on their behalf, how would brands need to change their business model?

Step 1 — Wind Tunnel

Strategic Stress-testing

Have you seen those videos where auto companies test car designs in wind tunnels? They expose the cars to all kinds of weather conditions and angles to see where the cars perform okay and where they break. That way, designers can fix inefficiencies before they become problems.

Strategic Wind Tunneling (see Figure 8.1) does the same thing for your strategy. Wind tunneling originates from scenario planning practices developed at Royal Dutch Shell, where strategies were stress-tested across multiple plausible futures to evaluate their robustness.[1]

Instead of hoping your strategy works in the future, you intentionally stress-test it against the scenarios I've just shared, some of which may seriously disrupt your plans.

What to do:

1. List your strategic pillars, initiatives or core bets as rows.
2. Place the four scenarios as columns.
3. For each intersection, assess whether the strategy:
   Works
   Works with improvements
   Fails

The main point is not to be extremely accurate, but to see where confidence breaks down.

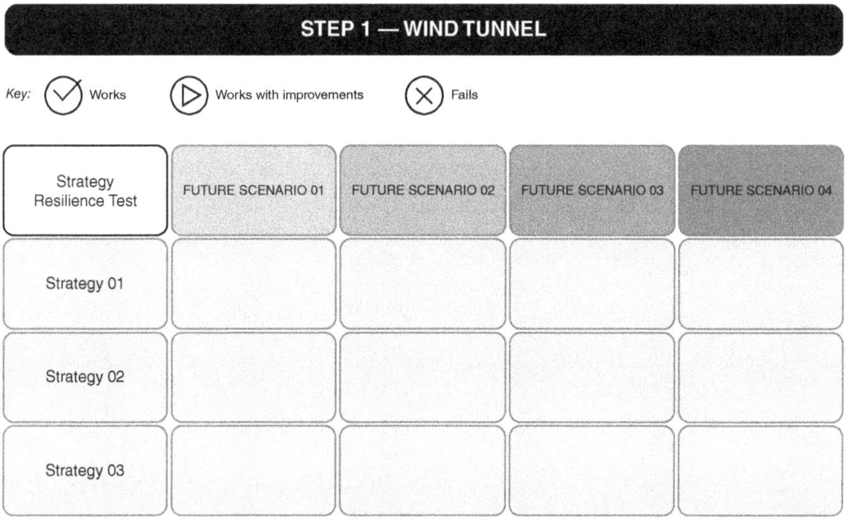

Figure 8.1 Strategic Wind Tunneling.

Company: global outdoor apparel brand
Time Horizon: five+ years
Context: strong brand equity, heavy dependence on premium wholesale distribution.

The leadership team runs the Wind Tunnel and maps their three pillars across the four future scenarios. As soon as the discussion starts, some interesting patterns begin to emerge.

Pillar 1: Premium wholesale retail distribution

In Future 4: The Algorithm Knows Best, the pillar consistently fails.

If AI agents select products based on price-to-value optimization, collaborative partnerships and efficiency scoring, shelf presence has no relevance. Retail visibility becomes secondary to algorithmic placement. Premium physical positioning offers no leverage. This is a big A-ha moment.

(continued)

(continued)

In Future 1: The Unconsumption Revolution, the same pillar strains once more. Premium positioning tied to aspirational pricing is very much scrutinized. Value is redefined not by margin but by contribution. Wholesale partners request lower volumes but higher accountability.

The pillar works in only one of the four futures. It strains in two. It fails in one.

That is definitely not resilience.

Pillar 2: Incremental seasonal product updates

In Future 2, where co-creation dominates, incremental improvement is viewed as passivity. Other brands invite customers into the innovation process and gain loyalty through participation. Seasonal updates feel transactional and very outdated. Everyone else that matters is already participating in culture and providing a platform to express identity through fashion.

In Future 3, where human craft regains status, incremental upgrades are acceptable but only if traceability exists.

This pillar works only with improvements in three of four futures. It fails nowhere outright, but it never performs strongly.

That is conditional strength, but certainly not robustness.

Pillar 3: Geographic expansion into emerging markets

In Future 1 and Future 3, geopolitical tightening and local-origin movements severely constrain expansion. In two scenarios, tariffs and social sentiment reduce margin to near zero.

The growth engine pillar repeatedly becomes exposure.

The team sits quietly. It's a realization that the strategy that they have all signed off on has to be improved. The Wind Tunnel revealed dependencies they had not quantified.

Two pillars collapse in at least one future.

One pillar survives only with significant adjustment.

The conclusion is not immediate redesign, but the current growth logic is limited and could be improved if the external conditions are considered.

Step 2 — Resilience Gap Finder

Finding Where Resilience Fails

Once you complete the Wind Tunnel, some weaknesses will be obvious.

The Resilience Gap Finder captures (see Figure 8.2):

- Where the strategy fails or only marginally holds.
- Which assumptions no longer stand.
- What becomes exposed.

> **Our strategy assumes** *[premium positioning in established retail channels will continue to drive growth]*,
> **but in Future** *[4: The Algorithm Knows Best]*
> **this no longer holds because** *[AI agents choose products based on algorithmic optimization rather than retail shelf visibility or brand presence.]*

This step turns intuition and assumptions into something discussable. Write down your responses to each of those three points.

Step 3 — Strategy Exposure Map

The Strategy Exposure Map (see Figure 8.3) helps you understand why the cracks exist.

For each exposed strategic element, ask:

- What is the pillar or bet?
- Why did it originally make sense?

STEP 2 — RESILIENCE GAP FINDER

GAP STATEMENT:

Our strategy assumes ______________________________,

but in Future ______________________________

this no longer holds because ______________________________.

Figure 8.2 Resilience Gap Finder.

- What assumptions does it rely on?
- What must remain true in the external world?
- Who or what does it depend on?

This tool surfaces the fragility of strategies that don't fail outright, but become irrelevant without anyone noticing.

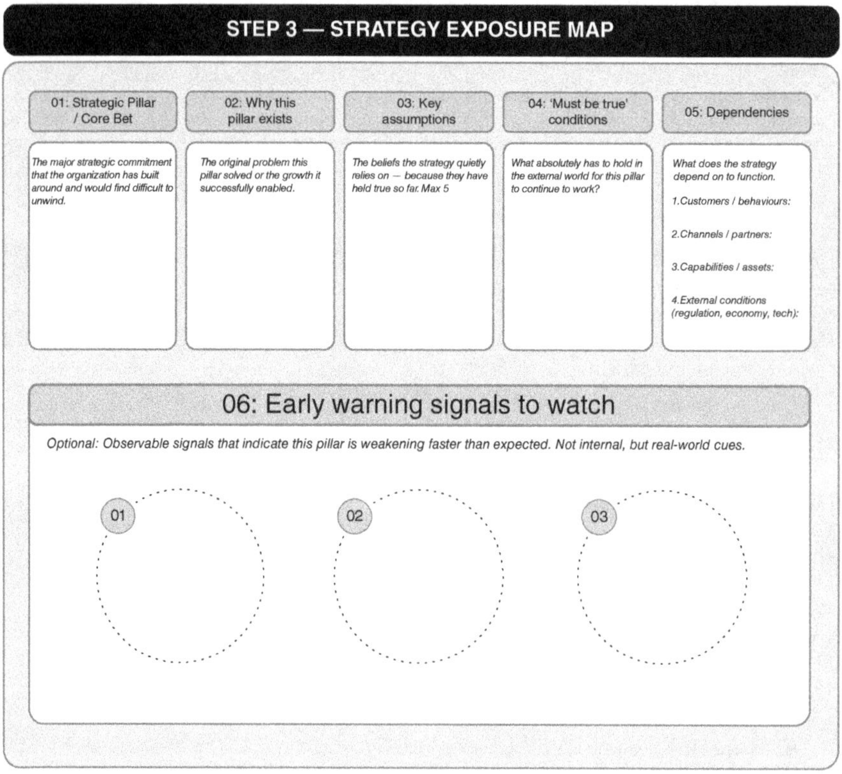

Figure 8.3 Strategy Exposure Map.

Step 4 — Resilience Action Ladder

Not every weakness requires immediate change.

The Resilience Action Ladder (see Figure 8.4) helps you decide how to respond:

1. No-regret bets: actions that strengthen the strategy across futures.
2. Options: small moves that preserve flexibility.
3. Trigger plans: actions activated when specific signals appear.

This allows you to adapt without overreacting.

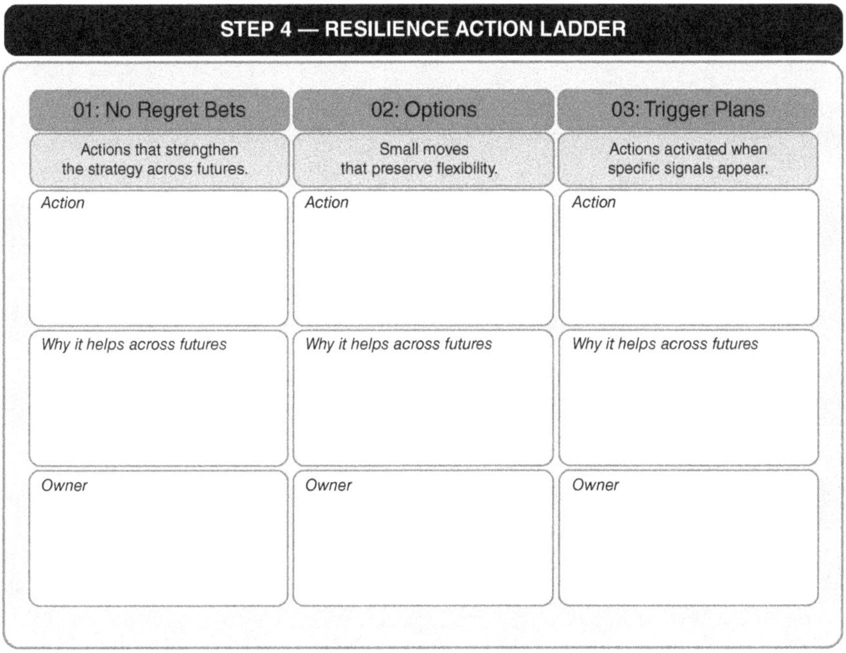

Trigger signals reviewed quarterly; *options reassessed annually.*

Figure 8.4 Resilience Action Ladder.

Common Pitfalls in Wind Tunneling

- Treating scenarios as predictions rather than stress tools.
- Defending legacy pillars emotionally.
- Overcorrecting based on one extreme scenario.
- Failing to define triggers after identifying weaknesses.

Remember, Wind Tunneling is a rehearsal, not forecasting.

What Your Wind Tunnel Results Set in Motion

Wind Tunneling does not end with foresight, it is meant to change posture.

Depending on what you discovered, you now face one of three realities.

If You Minimize the Findings

Short Term (0–12 Months) The existing strategy proceeds unchanged. Board confidence remains intact. Capital allocation continues along familiar paths.

Mid Term (1–3 Years) Weak pillars begin to require disproportionate support. Promotional spending increases. Retail negotiations tighten. Supply costs fluctuate. Internal debate intensifies, but correction still feels optional.

Long Term (3–5+ Years) Strategic rigidity becomes expensive. Growth slows unevenly across regions. Course correction requires structural change under performance pressure rather than strategic intent.

This shows us minimizing exposure preserves comfort but compounds fragility.

If You Reinforce Selectively

Short Term (0–12 Months) Leadership formally documents exposed assumptions. No-regret bets are initiated. Diversification begins quietly. Trigger thresholds are defined.

Mid Term (1–3 Years) Dependency decreases. Distribution channels diversify. Innovation logic becomes more participatory or structurally relevant. Exposure to single-scenario risk reduces.

Long Term (3–5+ Years) The strategy evolves gradually. Competitive resilience strengthens. Growth becomes less spectacular but more stable across conditions.

This demonstrates how selective reinforcement builds structural flexibility without abandoning identity.

If You Redesign Material Pillars

Short Term (0–12 Months) Internal resistance surfaces. Short-term targets may be recalibrated. Board discussions intensify. Organizational discomfort is visible.

Mid Term (1–3 Years) Growth logic realigns. Capital shifts toward pillars that survived stress-testing. Legacy dependencies shrink. Risk exposure rebalances.

Long Term (3–5+ Years) The company competes on foundations that persist across futures rather than on conditions that once existed.

Yes, having to redesign your strategy is disruptive, but not as disruptive as exposure to unexpected external shifts.

Reflection Prompts

- Which pillar did we defend most strongly and why?
- Which scenario felt most uncomfortable?
- Where are we structurally overdependent?
- If forced to rebuild from scratch, which pillar would we keep?

Answering these exposes attachment versus resilience.

What You Carry Forward into the Futures Strategy Canvas

From this Lab, record the outcomes of your strategy stress-test (see Figure 8.5).

Record the following:

- Strategy stress points.
- No-regret adaptations.
- Strategic options.
- Critical assumptions.
- Signals and triggers.

Nothing else moves forward.

This ensures the results are not stored as insight to be forgotten or overlooked, but incorporated directly into annual planning cycles, capital allocation discussions and board-level assumption reviews.

Under 'What Breaks'

Record only the strategic pillars or core bets that repeatedly failed or strained across scenarios.

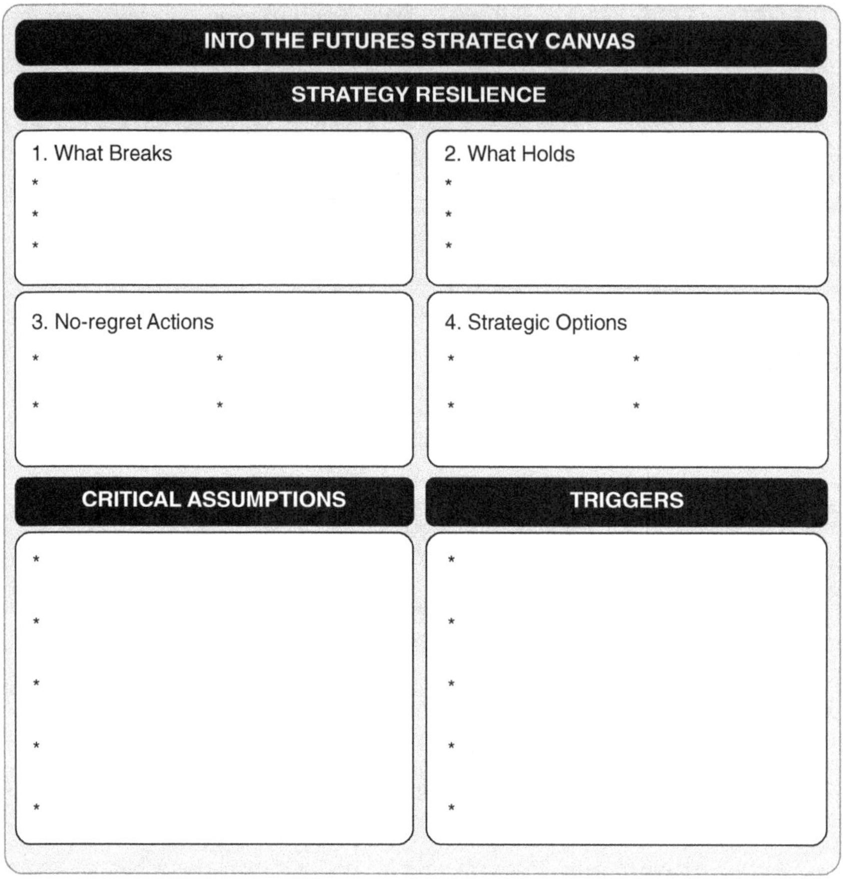

Figure 8.5 What You Carry Forward: Into the Futures Strategy Canvas.

Not everything that wobbled once.
Only what consistently weakens.
This may include:

- Overdependence on a dominant retail partner.
- Heavy reliance on premium perception as value proxy.
- Geographic expansion assumptions tied to political stability.
- Iterative innovation as the only growth engine.

Be specific and structural.

Under 'No-regret Adaptations'

Carry forward only the reinforcement actions you committed to through the Resilience Action Ladder.

These are moves that strengthen the strategy across multiple futures.

Examples:

- Diversifying channel exposure.
- Investing in traceability and supply chain visibility.
- Strengthening direct customer relationships.
- Building flexibility into product architecture.

If an action would make sense in three or more futures, it belongs here.

Under 'Options/Contingencies'

Document the conditional moves.

These are small, controlled steps that preserve flexibility without full redesign.

Examples:

- Running limited co-creation pilots.
- Testing localized production partnerships.
- Building capabilities in algorithmic commerce without full dependence.

They preserve optionality without commitment.

Under 'Critical Assumptions (3–5)'

Distill the three to five assumptions your strategy depends on most.

For example:

- Retail partners continue granting premium shelf space.
- Customers continue rewarding brand-led premium positioning.
- Emerging markets remain business-accessible.
- Incremental product improvement remains sufficient.

These assumptions should feel uncomfortable to write. That is the point.

Under 'Signals to Monitor' and 'Trigger Points'

For each assumption, define:

- A signal that would indicate weakening.
- A predefined action threshold.

For example:

- If premium shelf allocation drops below X% → accelerate direct-to-customer investment
- If local sourcing mandates pass in two priority markets → pause expansion plans
- If AI-mediated purchasing exceeds X% of sales → increase platform integration

This is where foresight becomes governance.

Continue Your Strategic Path

This Lab focused on stress-testing your strategy against potential future scenarios, finding the weaknesses and identifying how you can strengthen your strategy across multiple possible futures.

If your next question is about who your customer of the future might be, move to **Strategic Futures Lab 1**.

If uncertainty sits around whether your product will be relevant in the future, work through **Strategic Futures Lab 2**.

If the tension you feel relates to future risks and opportunities you must address today, go to **Strategic Futures Lab 3**.

If you want to know where the best opportunities for innovation lie, focus your attention on **Strategic Futures Lab 4.**

If you have completed all five Labs, continue to **Chapter 9** where you can complete your Futures Strategy Canvas.

Each Lab stands alone and they don't have to be completed in any particular order.

This is meant to be a choose-your-own-path playbook and you should follow the tension that feels most relevant for your organization.

PART III

From Choices to Capability

Even if you have not completed all the Labs by the time you turn to Part III, you have likely completed at least one of them and explored how changing your thinking can change the decisions in front of you.

In this final part of the book, we bring all five of the Futures Labs together into your Futures Strategy Canvas. This is where you will begin to see patterns you may have missed before and where you will learn how to connect what you have discovered through your rehearsals in the Labs to organisational capability.

But the journey does not end with your Futures Strategy Canvas. In fact, this is just the beginning. To truly benefit from futures intelligence, our entire organisational mindset needs to change. What the Labs and Futures Strategy Canvas provide is a mirror that shows us both how we make decisions as individuals and how decisions are made at an organisational level.

With this understanding, it then becomes easier to redesign entire corporate systems to better align with futures intelligence. This is not a one-and-done activity. It takes time, repetition and must be incorporated at every level: from individual leaders to teams to organisational priorities.

This is the essential work of Systems Learning in the world in which we now operate. I'll leave you with insights on how to develop a Systems Learning culture in your organisation and, in the process, how to develop organisational maturity that better prepares you for the future. Any future.

9 Create Your Own Futures Playbook

Complete your Futures Strategy Canvas and design your personalized futures system.

In this chapter you will find:

- **The Futures Strategy Canvas** (The main framework)
- **The Structure of the Futures Strategy Canvas**
- **Five Interconnected Layers** (Mapping the outputs of the five Strategic Futures Labs onto the Canvas)
- **How the Canvas Works as a System**
- **What the Canvas Ultimately Produces**

Up to this point, your choose-your-own-path journey has taken you through different Strategic Futures Labs. You have done the exercises, you have taken some brave decisions, and made trade-offs. Each of these Labs has asked you to explore a different strategic question under uncertainty. At the end of each of the Strategic Futures Labs you were prompted to note down the decision. Individually, each helps you make better decisions in their specific domain. However, when we put them together, they form a system.

A map of the future that can help us on our journey to building a resilient strategy. That system is the Futures Strategy Canvas.

If you did not complete every Lab, that is fine. The Playbook is designed to work in the same non-linear way as the book.

Here is the integration logic:

- Lab 1 gives you future worlds, future humans, priority needs, future barriers, relevance arenas and a strategic posture.
- Lab 2 gives you protect, adapt or phase-out decisions and the assumptions behind them.
- Lab 3 gives you your external posture in response to trends and outside influences: act, inform, option, deep dive, discard.
- Lab 4 gives you opportunity spaces worth exploring, and what you will explicitly deprioritize.
- Lab 5 gives you resilience results: what breaks, what holds, no-regret actions, strategic options, critical assumptions and triggers for change.

The Playbook is simply the system that holds these outputs together, so strategy becomes future-aware by design, not by occasional workshops.

The Futures Strategy Canvas

From foresight to choice, from choice to capability.

The Canvas is not a planning template. It is a decision architecture — a way to hold complexity without collapsing it into false certainty.

Why a Canvas and Not a Framework?

Traditional strategy frameworks assume a relatively stable environment, a single dominant future and linear cause–effect relationships.

The Futures Strategy Canvas assumes the opposite: multiple plausible futures and strategic hypotheses, incomplete information and therefore a living system that will update our futures intelligence at each critical decision-making point, decisions that must be made before clarity arrives.

The purpose of the Canvas is not to tell you what to do. It is to ensure that the choices you make are coherent, intentional and future-aware. It's there to prompt you to have the conversations, to apply the different lenses and to narrow focus on what would be most important for your organization in the future, considering the information we have today.

Layer 1: Future Humans & Needs

Strategic Futures Lab 1: Who Is My Customer of the Future?

Key Question Who are we truly designing for and under what future conditions?

What This Layer Anchors This layer defines relevance. It captures the future worlds, people, needs and barriers that shape where the organization should earn relevance. It prevents strategy from optimizing for yesterday's customer or assuming that needs remain static. It grounds every downstream decision in real future contexts. Real people, real constraints, real shifts in agency.

When this layer is weak, everything built on top of it may be operationally impressive but strategically misaligned.

Layer 2: Product and Value Relevance

Strategic Futures Lab 2: Will My Product Still Be Relevant?

Key Question Does what we offer today still matter in the futures we are preparing for? This can apply to individual products, services or broader product groups depending on the level at which the organization manages its portfolio.

What This Layer Anchors This layer protects against defending legacy offerings out of habit or attachment. It clarifies what needs evolution, what requires reinvention and what may require a deliberate exit.

When this layer is ignored, organizations protect products instead of protecting relevance.

Layer 3: Responsibility and Decision Posture

Strategic Futures Lab 3: What Future Risks and Opportunities Require Decisions Now?

Key Question Which external forces require ownership, and what is our intentional posture toward them?

What This Layer Anchors This layer transforms environmental uncertainty into explicit choices. It clarifies where the organization will act, where it will build options, where it will monitor and where it will consciously deprioritize.

Without this layer, external change remains abstract discussion rather than owned strategic direction.

Layer 4: Opportunity and Innovation Portfolio

Strategic Futures Lab 4: Where Are the Best Opportunities for Innovation?

Key Question Where should we explore, and where should we deliberately not?

What This Layer Anchors This layer converts uncertainty into disciplined optionality. It balances ambition with focus and prevents innovation from becoming reactive, scattered or symbolic.

When it's missing, innovation activity increases but strategic coherence decreases.

Layer 5: Strategy Resilience

Strategic Futures Lab 5: Will My Strategy Still Work in the Future?

Key Question How does our strategy perform across multiple plausible futures?

What This Layer Anchors This layer exposes fragility before performance does. It identifies stress points, no-regret actions, conditional bets and early warning signals tied to decision triggers.

Without this layer, strategy becomes a single bet disguised as confidence.

The Futures Strategy Canvas is designed to surface tensions you can address while it is still early and before it becomes too expensive to course correct. When customer futures are in conflict with your internal portfolio choices; when resilience tests reveal cracks in the strategies; when innovation ambitions don't match the risk posture, this will become clear in the Strategic Futures Lab exercises and has to be resolved before you map the strategy on the Canvas. It's not a friction you can smooth over. It's awareness. It's intelligence that helps you build a better strategic roadmap.

When used well, the Futures Strategy Canvas does a lot more than organize your thinking. It is a tool that can create a shared language across the organization and support future decision-making. It shows intention and that instills confidence in everyone working towards a common goal. The work that you are doing to complete the Canvas shines a light on explicit trade-offs made, no-regret actions, conditional bets tied to signals and triggers, how ambition and capability is aligned. It makes visible the decision patterns and blind spots. Its power lies in the fact that they are all made available, not buried in slide decks and budget meetings.

I have said this enough in this book, but the Canvas **does not predict** the future. It prepares you to engage with it coherently, systematically and intentionally. It's a living system that should be treated as such.

Example: A Completed Futures Strategy Canvas

The following example shows how the outputs from the five Strategic Futures Labs come together in the Futures Strategy Canvas.

This example uses the same **regional banking organization and personas introduced in Chapter 4, Lab 1**, demonstrating how insights from each Lab consolidate into one strategic view.

Company Context

Organization/Business Unit: mid-sized regional banking group
Industry/Category: financial services/retail banking
Strategic Horizon: 3–5 years
Current Positioning: trusted regional bank with strong SME and retail customer relationships.

The leadership team runs the Strategic Futures Labs during a strategy offsite to test whether their current strategy will remain relevant in a changing financial environment.

Future Humans & Needs (Lab 1)

Future Worlds Considered

- Frictionless but Opaque.
- High Friction, Low Trust.

- Identity & Belonging First.
- Managed Scarcity.

These futures place different pressures on how people make financial decisions.

Future Humans/Personas

- **Maya – The Delegator** (relies on automated financial tools).
- **Arjun – The Verifier** (independently checks institutional claims).
- **Sofia – The Ethical Investor** (aligns financial choices with values).
- **Wei – The Responsible Planner** (prioritizes long-term stability).

These personas illustrate how financial decision-making may evolve across different future conditions.

Tier 1 Needs

- Trust & fairness.
- Safety & security.

Across the scenarios, these needs appear repeatedly, indicating they are structurally important for the bank's relevance.

Key Future Barriers

- Opaque algorithmic financial decisions.
- Declining trust in financial institutions.
- Pressure for ethical capital allocation.

Future Relevance Arenas

- Transparent AI-driven financial decision infrastructure.
- Community-aligned lending and investment.
- Public impact disclosure for financial products.

Strategic Posture

Adjust The leadership team keeps the core banking model but expands capabilities around transparency and responsible finance.

Product Posture (Lab 2)

The team evaluates whether their current offerings remain relevant under future conditions.

Protect

Products that remain structurally relevant.

- Core savings accounts.
- Current account services.
- SME lending services.

Adapt

Products where the need persists but the form must evolve.

- Automated financial advisory tools with transparent decision logic.
- Investment products with transparent impact scoring.

Phase Out

Products that risk undermining trust.

- Opaque investment bundles with complex fee structures.

Responsibility Posture (Lab 3)

The team evaluates external forces shaping the financial industry.

Act

External shifts requiring immediate ownership.

- AI governance and transparency standards for automated decisions.
- Transparent lending criteria and reporting.

Option

Areas explored through controlled experimentation.

- Community-driven lending pools.

Discard

Areas offering limited strategic advantage.

- Highly immersive digital banking environments that do not improve financial decision-making.

Opportunity Spaces (Lab 4)

Selected Opportunity Spaces

- Explainable AI financial advisory systems.
- Impact-transparent investment portfolios.
- Community-driven capital allocation tools.

Explicitly Deprioritized Spaces

- Speculative digital asset products without clear customer value.

These decisions help the organization focus innovation resources where they are most aligned with future customer needs.

Strategy Resilience (Lab 5)

The strategy is then stress-tested across multiple future scenarios.

What Breaks

- Opaque automated financial decisions.
- Fee-driven product structures.

What Holds

- Institutional trust when transparency improves.
- Regional relationship banking.

No-regret Actions

Actions that strengthen the strategy across futures.

- Introduce explainability layers in AI-supported advisory tools.
- Publish transparent reporting on lending and investment impact.

Strategic Options

Moves that preserve flexibility.

- Customer-controlled algorithmic financial advisors.
- Community-directed investment funds.

Critical Assumptions

- Customers will increasingly expect transparency in financial decisions.
- AI will play a growing role in financial decision-making.
- Trust will remain a differentiating factor in financial services.

Triggers

Signals that would trigger strategic action.

- If AI-mediated financial advice exceeds 30% of new investment decisions → accelerate explainability capabilities.
- If regulation mandates transparency for financial algorithms → expand governance and reporting.
- If demand for ethical investment products exceeds 20–25% of portfolio demand → scale impact-based offerings.

Result

The completed Futures Strategy Canvas (Figure 9.1) allows the leadership team to clearly see:

- Where future relevance may emerge.
- Which products must evolve.
- Which external forces require action.
- Where innovation should be focused.
- How resilient the strategy is across multiple futures.

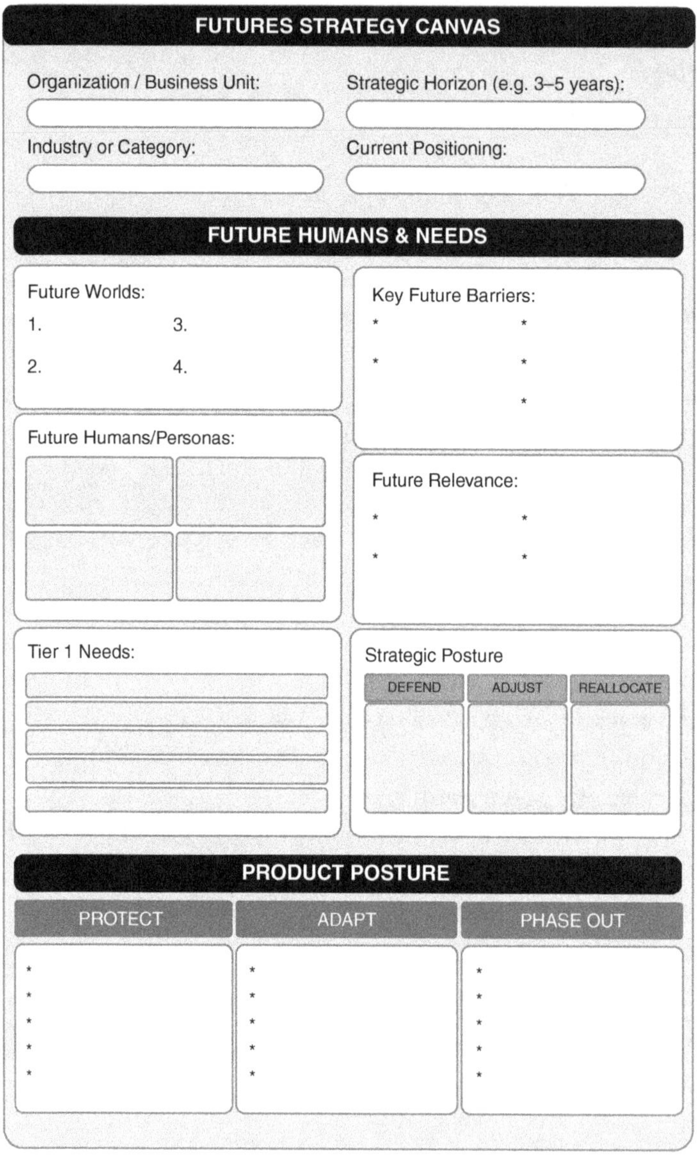

Figure 9.1 Futures Strategy Canvas.

FUTURES FORWARD

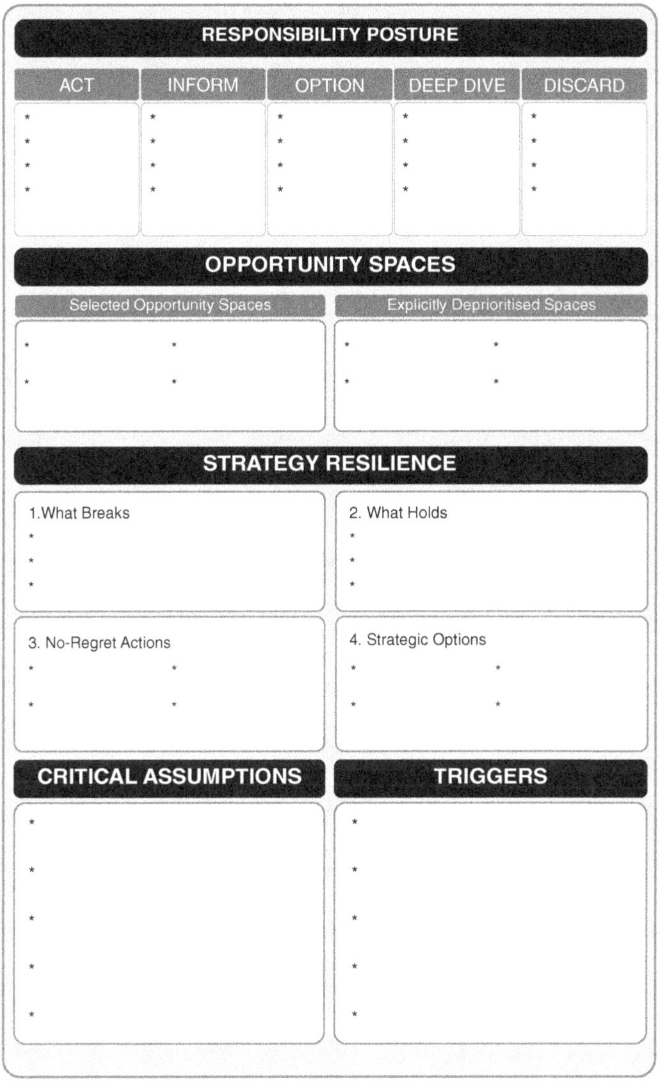

Figure 9.1 (*Continued*)

Rather than predicting the future, the Canvas creates a structured way to prepare for it.

Each posture in the Futures Strategy Canvas operates at a different level of strategic decision-making.

Strategic posture clarifies where the organization should earn relevance in the future by determining how strongly it should shift attention toward emerging customer needs.

Product posture determines how the existing portfolio must evolve in response to those needs.

Responsibility posture defines how the organization responds to external forces such as regulation, technology shifts or societal pressure.

Together these postures ensure that customer relevance, portfolio decisions and external response remain aligned.

How to Keep This Alive

A Futures Playbook only becomes a capability when it has a cadence. A simple operating rhythm is enough:

- Monthly: signal review and trigger check. What assumptions weakened? What is emerging?
- Quarterly: portfolio option review. What are we preserving, testing or closing?
- Biannually: refresh future humans and needs. Are we still designing for the right people in the right conditions?
- Annually: wind tunnel the strategy again, then update the Canvas.

You can ensure disciplined re-evaluation and staying on top of any potential threats.

Your Futures Strategy Canvas

Use this space to note down what you have learned from each of the Labs and build an assessment of your Futures Playbook into your organization's operating rhythm as I described earlier.

10 What Your Choices Reveal

Decision patterns, risk posture, bias and strategic tendencies.

By the time you reach this chapter, you have already gone through something that most strategy books never ask you to do. You have been forced to make choices under uncertainty. Not just in theory, but real decisions about where to focus your attention, which questions you answered with urgency, which ones felt less relevant and which ones you were hoping you didn't have to answer.

You have now explored future customers and their needs. You have tested product relevance, explored which trends could bring the highest risk, and possibly the highest rewards. You mapped innovation opportunity areas. And finally, you have stress-tested your strategy.

But here is the thing, while you were doing that, even though each Lab asked a specific question, all of them together also revealed how you decide in the context of uncertainty.

What you chose matters, of course, but what matters even more is ***how*** you chose.

Strategic failure doesn't usually begin with lack of information or poor intelligence. Instead it stems from predictable thinking patterns, used instinctively when the pressure arrives. The Strategic Futures Labs were designed not only to help you through the thought process and make decisions, but also to surface those patterns and raise your awareness of them.

In this chapter, I aim to help you identify your decision style, so that you can watch out for the blind spots. And this isn't an easy task, because individual style and corporate context and risk posture are two different things. I understand that there might be a tension between what risks you are ready to take as an individual versus what the organization you are part of may allow.

But the objective here isn't to focus on these differences. It is to highlight the blind spots you have to prepare for, whatever the risk profile is. We may not be able to eliminate blind spots, but we can manage them by awareness. Once you understand your default posture, you gain the ability to shift it when the external environment demands us to act differently.

What this chapter adds is a bridge. The Labs helped you make choices and now this chapter helps you translate those choices into strategic meaning. That translation happens in three steps:

- First, name what your choices reveal about your default decision posture under pressure.
- Second, identify the assumptions hiding beneath those choices.
- Third, decide what the organization should change as a result, not in theory, but in governance, resource allocation and the triggers you will use to course-correct.

If the Futures Labs were the dress rehearsal, then this chapter is the debrief. It goes from 'What did we choose?' to 'What does that say about how we run strategy, and what needs to shift next?'

Why Foresight Alone Rarely Changes Behaviour

This book is focused on trying to help teams and leaders close the Decision Gap. This is one of the biggest frustrations in foresight and strategy work. How do we move from ***knowing*** to ***doing*** based on the new information we have and not snap back to our old, comfortable patterns.

Behavioural science has remained remarkably consistent on this point — humans do not respond to information in a linear way. Under uncertainty, we rely more heavily on cognitive shortcuts, emotional cues and identity-protecting narratives. The higher the stakes, the stronger this effect becomes.

Information is an invaluable resource. It can change our awareness, but it doesn't automatically change what feels psychologically or professionally safe. In corporate settings, every decision is filtered not only through the simple individual logic, but through perceived career risk, social belonging, and the invisible rules of what is rewarded now and in the future. This is why foresight often illuminates the future, but it rarely changes the behaviour in the present. We tend to blame foresight for being a faulty practice and try to force-fit it into a system that isn't working to satisfy the needs of its users. But that seems like a topic for another book. Let's focus on working with the current systems for now and improving our decision-making incrementally.

Research in behavioural decision science shows that heuristics and biases shape judgement precisely when decisions matter most, not least.[1]

Heuristics are mental shortcuts that are deployed under uncertain, complex or incomplete context to help the brain make decisions quickly.[2]

This means the problem is rarely a lack of intelligence. It is that uncertainty changes how the brain prioritizes safety and control, as well as belonging, which is also a driving factor when making choices as part of a corporate culture. Deviation from the common belief can have career implications and often the innovators and the foresight practitioners are the challengers in the room.

Two Forces Behind Every Strategic Choice

Across the Labs, two underlying forces quietly shaped how you engaged with the questions.

The first force is your tolerance for uncertainty. Some people are energized by ambiguity. Others experience it as a threat. Neuroscience research shows that uncertainty, especially when the future outcomes are ambiguous, activates regions of the brain that are involved in the processing of stress and threat (the amygdala and insula). This activation is associated with altered decision-making strategies and biased judgements under uncertainty.[3]

The second is your orientation toward loss versus opportunity. Daniel Kahneman and Amos Tversky demonstrated decades ago that people experience losses more intensely than the equivalent gains. This is a phenomenon called loss aversion.[4]

In strategic contexts, this often makes inaction feel rational and safe, even when it quietly increases the long-term risk.

When these two forces interact, they produce recognizable decision patterns.

These are not fixed personality traits: these forces can and do fluctuate with the change in context. Once credibility and political capital increase, uncertainty tolerance often expands. And vice versa — the sensitivity to loss increases when performance pressure rises. This is important to understand, in fact it is probably one of the most important traits of a leader. Namely that a leader's leadership style should not remain constant. It should be a flexible, context-dependent posture that shifts for the optimal results.

- When uncertainty feels threatening and loss dominates attention, organizations optimize instead of explore. They demand excessive proof, favour incremental gains and treat bold reallocation as reckless.
- When uncertainty is tolerated, but loss aversion continues to remain strong, experimentation becomes cautious and reversible.
- When the desire for opportunity dominates but uncertainty tolerance continues to be low, organizations chase signals without discipline.

The only way for genuine strategic exploration to take place is if ambiguity is accepted and loss is reframed as learning.

The Decision Posture Matrix

Rather than thinking in terms of personality types, it is more useful to think in terms of decision postures (see Figure 10.1). These are situational patterns that emerge when people and organizations face uncertainty time and time again.

This is the simple matrix. Each quadrant of this matrix produces a characteristic decision posture that appears repeatedly in organizations under pressure.

On one axis sits tolerance for uncertainty, ranging from low to high. On the other sits orientation toward loss or opportunity. Where you tend to operate on this map influences how you interpreted each Lab.

Before you label a choice as 'good' or 'bad', test it for resilience. A choice is only as strong as the future conditions it assumes.

Here is a simple way to stress-test any decision you made in the Labs:

1. Write the choice in one line.
2. List the three assumptions that must hold for it to be right.
3. Run those assumptions across at least three plausible futures. Ask: does this assumption still hold, weaken or reverse?
4. If an assumption breaks, do not debate harder. Design one of three responses:
   - A no-regret reinforcement that helps in most futures.
   - An option that keeps flexibility without full commitment.
   - A trigger that tells you when to shift course.

This is also how your choices become usable inside the Futures Strategy Canvas. The Canvas is not just a record of what you decided. It is a system that makes assumptions visible, and ties them to actions, options and triggers so you can adapt without waiting for certainty.

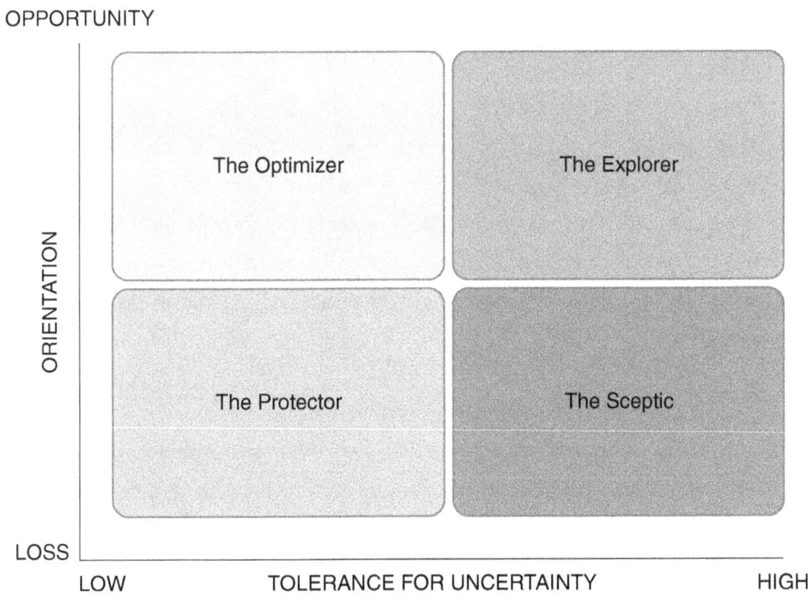

Figure 10.1 The Decision Posture Matrix.

Four Common Decision Postures

The Protector When uncertainty feels threatening and losses loom large, decisions tend to centre around preservation of the status quo. In the Strategic Futures Labs, this posture would have shown up as a strong attachment to current customers, discomfort with questioning product relevance and a preference for incremental innovation. The underlying logic is, of course, understandable: protect what works now, avoid visible failure by risking too much, maintain credibility.

This posture is reinforced by well-documented biases such as status quo bias and the sunk cost fallacy, which make existing commitments feel safer than unfamiliar alternatives.

The blind spot to watch out for is subtle. And dangerous! By the time you spot the erosion, it is often quite advanced, so actions will tend to be taken in a state of emergency, reactively, rather than by design.

When you hear the following phrases repeatedly — 'We need more proof', 'Now is not the time' — you should stop and reflect on whether they might be warning signs. Are they prudent or are they starting to accumulate into a delayed response to a situation? In moments of volatility, the role of the Protector is invaluable, but in some situations, when it is necessary to work with fundamental changes, overprotection is actually a survival risk.

A high-stakes example of this shows up in capital allocation decisions.

Imagine a global manufacturing company facing early signals of tightening regulation on product repairability. The Protector posture often responds by defending the current model: preserve margin, protect the supply chain, keep the product roadmap intact. The choice sounds disciplined.

But when the leadership team runs the stress test, the hidden assumptions surface quickly:

- Regulation will remain fragmented and slow.
- Customers will prioritize price and features over repairability.
- Retail partners will absorb the pressure without changing shelf rules.

Across multiple plausible futures, those assumptions do not hold reliably. In one future, repairability becomes a baseline requirement. In another, retailers use repairability scores to control visibility. In a third, brand trust collapses after a public backlash tied to waste.

The revised decision is not 'go all in on repairability tomorrow'. It becomes conditional strategy:

- A no-regret move: redesign packaging and parts documentation for transparency.
- An option: pilot modular components in one region.
- A trigger: if two priority markets pass repairability laws within 18 months, accelerate the product architecture shift.

Same team, same data, different posture, better strategy.

The Optimizer Some leaders and decision-makers appear comfortable pursuing opportunity, but this is true only within a budgeted risk, where the boundaries of uncertainty are mapped. They are very enthusiastic about efficiency gains, optimization and incremental innovation of the existing products, processes and business models.

In the Strategic Futures Labs, this posture often appeared as interest in Horizon 2 opportunities, provided there was a credible business case and measurable and controllable upside.

This approach can really thrive in operating environments where there are established KPIs and short planning cycles. The risk here is in the belief that disruption can be optimized away. Sometimes refinement is simply not enough to compensate for structural change.

Optimizers often assume that external shifts can be neutralized by better metrics, better sequencing or better execution. That is why they tend to overly rely on historical data to make big assumptions about future success and believe that small changes will protect them from disruption. That might be the case in stable environments, but I think by now everyone agrees, this is not the environment in which we operate, so this model could simply lose relevance.

A pivotal example of this shows up in customer acquisition strategy.

Imagine a global streaming platform facing early signals that AI assistants may soon begin recommending and selecting entertainment services on behalf of users. The Optimizer posture often responds by refining the current model: optimize recommendation algorithms, improve pricing tiers and run experiments to increase retention and engagement. The choice sounds disciplined.

But when the leadership team runs the stress test, the hidden assumptions surface quickly:

- Customers will continue making subscription decisions themselves.
- Brand loyalty will remain a primary driver of platform selection.
- AI intermediaries will not fundamentally alter how entertainment services are discovered.

Across multiple plausible futures, those assumptions do not hold reliably. In one future, AI assistants automatically bundle and switch streaming services based on user preferences. In another, device manufacturers integrate entertainment ecosystems directly into hardware. In a third, algorithmic curation weakens brand differentiation.

The revised decision is not 'abandon optimization tomorrow'. It becomes conditional strategy:

- A no-regret move: improve interoperability with external platforms and AI assistants.
- An option: pilot partnerships with device ecosystems to test integrated content delivery.
- A trigger: if AI-mediated subscription selection exceeds a defined threshold, accelerate ecosystem integration.

Same team, same data, different posture, better strategy.

The Explorer In cases where uncertainty is well tolerated and the priority is on seeking opportunity, true exploration becomes possible.

This posture would show up in the Labs as deep engagement with future personas, enthusiasm for Horizon 3 opportunities, and comfort with scenario thinking.

Research into expert judgement supports this mindset. Philip Tetlock's work on superforecasting shows that the most effective forecasters remain curious, probabilistic and willing to revise their views as new information emerges.

In his large 'prediction tournaments', those who repeatedly outperform others did not rely on certainty. Instead, they incrementally updated their beliefs, treated futures as a continuum of probabilities rather than fixed outcomes, and actively sought evidence against confirmation bias.

This mindset, based on probabilities that tolerates ambiguity while continuously refining judgement, is aligned with the same behaviours that help effective organizational foresight and futures intelligence.[5]

The risk here is that if we don't do the execution, we may end up with strategy theatre and nothing else. The Explorer can underestimate the inertia in an organization, along with the headwinds, the political constraints and the difficulty to translate foresight into action.

Exploration without integration creates this failure mode: insight and foresight accumulates, multiple future scenarios are explored, systems are built, signals are monitored, but none of this is acted upon, because the organizational mechanisms and processes needed to facilitate this change remain as they are and turn into blockers. Curiosity alone is not enough.

A critical example of this shows up in emerging technology investment.

Imagine a consumer electronics company noticing early signals that ambient computing could reduce the importance of individual devices. The Explorer posture often responds by launching experimental initiatives: voice-first interfaces, shared device ecosystems and partnerships with smart-home infrastructure providers. The intention is to learn early and position the company for future opportunities. The choice sounds visionary.

But when the leadership team runs the stress test, the hidden assumptions surface quickly:

- Customers will become comfortable interacting with invisible computing systems.
- Value will shift from standalone devices to connected ecosystems.
- Hardware differentiation alone will not sustain long-term competitive advantage.

Across multiple plausible futures, those assumptions evolve unevenly. In one future, privacy concerns slow adoption. In another, ecosystem fragmentation prevents dominant platforms from emerging. In a third, regulatory scrutiny changes how connected systems are deployed.

The revised decision is not 'scale every experiment immediately'. It becomes conditional strategy:

- A no-regret move: invest in interoperability standards across product categories.
- An option: pilot ecosystem-based services in a limited number of markets.
- A trigger: if ecosystem-based purchasing exceeds a defined threshold, expand platform investment.

Same curiosity, same ambition, different posture, stronger strategy.

The Sceptic This posture combines the tolerance to uncertainty with awareness of risk and downside. Sceptics usually rigorously question assumptions, engage deeply in stress-testing and resist premature commitments.

In the Strategic Futures Labs, this often showed up as strong engagement with Wind Tunnelling, sense-checking and testing organizational readiness.

This posture belongs to decision-makers who have experienced failures in transformation. The biggest blind spot here is delay. This excessive double checking and caution could become an own form of risk.

A high-profile example of this shows up in infrastructure transformation decisions.

Imagine a global logistics company evaluating whether to deploy autonomous delivery vehicles. Early signals suggest strong long-term potential, but regulatory approval, infrastructure readiness and public acceptance remain uncertain. The Sceptic posture often responds by slowing the decision: commissioning further analysis, running controlled pilots and closely monitoring policy developments. The choice sounds prudent.

But when the leadership team runs the stress test, the hidden assumptions surface quickly:

- Regulatory approval will expand gradually across major markets.
- Autonomous technology will reach reliability levels suitable for commercial logistics.
- Public acceptance will not significantly delay deployment.

Across multiple plausible futures, those assumptions evolve differently. In some regions regulation accelerates rapidly. In others, safety concerns trigger delays. In a third, competitors move faster and reshape market expectations.

The revised decision is not 'reject the technology'. It becomes conditional strategy:

- A no-regret move: build internal expertise on autonomous logistics systems.
- An option: launch pilot programmes in regulatory-friendly markets.
- A trigger: if two major logistics markets approve autonomous commercial operations, expand deployment.

Same caution, same discipline, different posture, better strategy.

This Is About Systems, Not Personality It is tempting to label these postures as personal traits, but that would be a mistake.

Organizational behaviour research shows the influence of context on the individual decision-making disposition. Incentives, governance structures, career risk and cultural norms all influence which postures are rewarded and which are suppressed, and they are just as important as individual postures.[6]

When short-term certainty signals are rewarded, even the high uncertainty-tolerant leaders will gradually narrow their exploration, or they will leave and find an environment that matches their risk tolerance and ambitions more closely. If the company penalizes long-term exploration, then it is logical that protective posture will surface. I am not saying this is done intentionally, but this happens where the structural processes are built for short-term reward. In this case, systemic reinforcement will override individual preference and the Decision Gap becomes embedded into the system.

How many times have you heard your own organization praised externally for qualities you don't really see unfolding in the same way internally? Many companies are celebrated publicly for exploration and innovation, while internally they structurally reward exploitation of current ideas, safeguarding perceived certainty and protecting the current products and systems. When that is the case, the Decision Gap is systemic rather than personal.

Which of these postures has historically led to leadership promotion and which has led to exits? The answers to these questions often reveal more about your organization's true strategic posture than any published vision, mission and innovation statements.

Decision Debrief Exercise

Choose one decision you made in any Strategic Futures Lab. Then answer these five questions in writing.

1. What did we choose, in one sentence?
2. What were we trying to protect: performance, reputation, control or option value?
3. What did we assume would stay stable? List three assumptions.
4. What would have to be true in the external world for our choice to remain correct?
5. If that stability is not guaranteed, what is our response?
   - Reinforce with a no-regret move.
   - Preserve flexibility with an option.
   - Define a trigger that forces re-evaluation.

If you cannot answer these cleanly, the decision is not yet strategic, it's only a preference.

Seeing Your Organization in the Mirror

The question Chapter 10 leaves you with is this:

> *If uncertainty increases tomorrow, what would your organization default to: protection, optimization, exploration or scepticism? And even more importantly, is that the required posture for the future you are preparing for or do you need to reconsider?*

If you trace back your answers in the five Labs, they led to this answer. This was a hidden test that enables you to slow down and think about it in the comfort of this simulation of real-life conditions, so that you can act with knowledge, awareness and conviction once real strategic decisions are required.

A Short Pause Before Moving On

Before you continue, I suggest you also answer this question:

> *When certainty disappears, what do you instinctively try to protect first: Reputation, control, possibility?*

It's not a one-answer-fits-all situation. It's informative to answer this on your own behalf, but also from the perspective of the entire C-suite. This will identify the automatic defensive posture for you and every other decision-maker. This can surface the friction patterns between what each stakeholder will protect instinctively as a priority. It will also reveal where alignment is strong.

Most of the executive conflict is not about information or even intent. It's usually about competing priorities, in this case protection priorities under uncertainty. If one leader is protecting control, another is protecting reputation and a third is protecting possibility, then they are optimizing for different definitions of risk. When we understand this, what looks like a disagreement on strategy is often disagreement on what should not be lost.

Where This Takes You Next

This chapter is not asking you to become a different kind of person, but it is asking you to become a different kind of organization.

If Chapter 10 helped you see your defaults, Chapter 11 focuses on how to redesign the decision environment so better choices become easier to make. That means team practices, meeting design, psychological safety and leadership behaviours that make futures intelligence usable, not just an option.

This is what will allow you to turn the Futures Strategy Canvas you created in Chapter 9 into a repeatable operating system within your organization. Once you have understood your defaults and redesigned your internal environment to aid better decision-making, the Futures Strategy Canvas becomes the place where decisions, assumptions, options and triggers live together, so strategy can evolve without losing coherence.

If you want to understand how to shape decision environments that support better choices under uncertainty, Chapter 11 explores how futures intelligence should be embedded into teams, processes and governance. This is the point at which you can turn everything you have learned into a coherent, repeatable system. Are you ready?

11 Building Futures Intelligence in Teams

Practical ways to embed foresight into culture, processes, leadership and governance.

It's very clear by now that neither lack of imagination about the future, nor information about emerging signals are the missing piece. Neither are they the main problem organizations face.The problem is that whatever foresight they generate internally or commission externally struggles to survive contact with everyday decision-making: meetings, incentives, reporting cycles, quarterly pressure, short-term ROI, internal politics and difference in what stakeholders must protect.

Chapter 10 surfaced how decision patterns form under uncertainty. In this chapter I want to address what comes next, after these patterns become visible.

This chapter follows a simple progression.

First, the foundation: what needs to be true in the team environment for futures intelligence to survive?

Second, the practices: what teams do differently week to week.
Third, the leadership behaviours: what leaders must consistently model and reward.
Finally, measurement: how do you know futures intelligence is becoming a real capability, not just theatre?

And that's one of the biggest questions in corporate foresight — how do you design an organization that can engage with the future without oversimplifying, rejecting new ideas and slowly defaulting back to what feels safe, but is potentially more risky?

I don't want you to perceive this chapter as one that will tell you exactly how to set up a foresight function. It isn't. I want to focus this chapter on providing my perspective on how to build futures intelligence as an organizational capability, which makes it something that shapes decisions even when no one explicitly says the word 'foresight'. That has been possibly one of the biggest learnings of my decade-long futures career. Don't force the method into a system that won't absorb it. Instead, hack the system, hack the method and find where it could be embedded painlessly.

Otherwise, it simply won't work and you will find yourself in the futures forums preaching the academically right concepts, arguing about what foresight is and how it should be done properly, but you will never have the traction in a real business that is faced with, yes, an outdated system of incentives and purpose and possibly very traditional leadership. Let's do something about it. This is about doing whatever we can to gain a step further, not pushing with the wrong narrative and the right intention. Good intentions won't matter, because under such conditions change just won't happen.

Why Foresight Breaks When It Lives in a Team

In response to uncertainty, many organizations create specialist units: foresight teams, innovation labs, trend functions. These steps are well intentioned, but sometimes they prove disappointing. Teams can be incredibly good at what they do, but because the function of innovation or foresight is being isolated, this sends a signal that there is this 'special unit' that will manage uncertainty for us on the periphery and we won't have to change our ways here, at the core.

Research into corporate foresight shows that when futures work is structurally separated from core decision processes, its impact remains limited. Insights are generated, but they arrive either too early to feel relevant or too late to alter direction. They are seen as interesting, but not binding.

Yes, specialist teams do generate insight. They can even generate foresight, but if the governance structures, incentives and reporting lines remain unchanged, this foresight will always struggle to translate into strategic action.

Does this pattern sound familiar? Impressive presentations, wow! Great workshops, very engaging, followed by ambitious roadmaps, and then … a return to business as usual.

When the foresight function is separated from the resource allocation, from the performance measurement and away from executive accountability, it becomes an advisory function rather than a lens to add to the decision-making process. Yes, it will inspire and inform conversations, but will it shift commitments and capital allocation? Probably not.

This here is an integration problem, and no professional training in foresight will solve it.

I think that having an isolated foresight function could even deepen the Decision Gap, because of perceived future-readiness, just because the work exists *somewhere*. Meanwhile, the core business units continue to optimize on the basis of yesterday, believing that tomorrow will be quite similar. In this scenario, while exploitation remains rewarded, exploration, if it happens at all, does so merely symbolically.

This dynamic creates frustration on both ends — foresight teams feel unheard and lose motivation; operational leaders feel exposed to (and even pressured by) ideas that seem unrealistic within the current constrained operating environment. No one is wrong, but no one is able to progress in unison, either. System redesign is needed to allow for ambiguity.

So in my mind, embedding futures intelligence is a lot more than just adding a new team. The organization has to support how capital is allocated, how success is measured, how decisions are made, how risks are framed and mitigated.

Until that happens, foresight remains a function and when it does, foresight becomes a capability.

This distinction aligns with research confirming that corporate foresight operates as a microfoundation of dynamic capabilities. Foresight strengthens organizational adaptability only when it enhances managerial cognition and resource reconfiguration processes.[1] In this sense, foresight has to become capability-building **infrastructure** rather than an analytical add-on.

This pattern is well documented in the work of René Rohrbeck and Menes Kum, who ran one of the most comprehensive studies of corporate foresight to date and whose research shows that foresight contributes to performance only when it is embedded in strategy, governance and leadership processes, not when it exists as an isolated activity. When it is embedded, they found that firms with high foresight maturity systematically outperformed their peers in profitability and market capitalization.[2,3]

In other words, futures intelligence creates value when it changes decisions, not when it produces foresight.

In short, foresight fails when it is treated as a content problem rather than a capability problem.

Empirical research into corporate foresight maturity helps clarify why. These are the three stages that an organization usually goes through as the foresight capability evolves.

1. **Peripheral foresight:** trend reports, ad hoc scenario workshops, innovation isolated at the edge.
2. **Coordinated foresight:** formal scanning linked to strategy discussions, limited executive integration.
3. **Embedded foresight:** systematic integration into capital allocation, portfolio management and leadership dialogue.[4]

The difference between these three stages is not how much imagination is deployed, what type of analytical superiority or the level of methodological quality. At its core, it is the organization's foundational, structural commitment that determines the extent to which foresight shapes real decisions.

Only then does futures intelligence become consequential. Without the integration, it continues to live simply as a commentary. An interesting, innovative, sparking ideas conversation … but still just a commentary.

From Foresight to Intelligence

One part of the issue is also the framing of foresight and the expectation of the organization as to what foresight is meant to deliver.

These three layers, often collapsed into one, hold a very important distinction:

- **Foresight:** these are the signals, trends, scenarios, future outlooks and perspectives.
- **Futures intelligence:** the ability to interpret the foresight and connect it to choices.
- **Futures capability:** the organizational conditions that allow intelligence to influence action.

Most organizations invest heavily in the first layer and assume the rest will follow. But without consistent and intentional effort and support, this is not possible.

Research on corporate foresight consistently defines foresight not merely as scanning or scenario development, but as a process that includes triggering organizational responses to change.[5] Without this response dimension, insight remains inert.

Similarly, studies on the roles of corporate foresight show that foresight contributes to innovation and performance only when it influences strategy formulation, portfolio evaluation and governance processes — not when it remains confined to analysis.[6]

UNESCO's concept of futures literacy sharpens the same distinction: futures literacy is not about knowing more about the future, but about using anticipatory thinking to improve present decisions.[7]

The shift from insight generation to decision use is the real work of futures intelligence.

The Four Conditions Futures Intelligence Requires

What are the conditions under which futures intelligence could actually shape decisions? In drawing from personal experience, foresight research, organizational studies and behavioural science, I have found that there are four key conditions nurturing success.

Allowing Space for Uncertainty Many organizations claim they value long-term thinking, while in fact they reward certainty, speed of execution and data that provides confidence. Uncertainty may be discussed but it's only done so theoretically and in practice, it is actually punished.

Behavioural research shows that when uncertainty is framed as incompetence or risk, people narrow their thinking and revert to familiar patterns. This dynamic has been well established in organizational research on threat rigidity. It demonstrates the fact that under conditions of perceived threat, organizations and individuals narrow their thinking and revert back to familiar, well-learned routines rather than exploring new alternatives.[8]

Empirical research of companies who engage in exploration under uncertainty shows that experimentation only persists where ambiguity is structurally legitimized.[9] On the other hand, organizations that prematurely penalize uncertainty suppress the adaptive behaviours needed for long-term renewal.

Building futures intelligence requires treating uncertainty as a legitimate working condition, not as a temporary failure of analysis. Leaders need these explicit safe spaces where it is acceptable to say, 'We don't know yet, but here is what we are observing and this is what it ***may*** lead to'.

What leaders do matters more than what they say. In practice, futures intelligence grows when leaders consistently do five things:

1. Ask for assumptions before forecasts. 'What must be true for this plan to work?'
2. Legitimize uncertainty in the room. 'We do not know yet' becomes acceptable language.
3. Protect options from premature ROI demands, especially early experiments.
4. Reward signal surfacing, not just certainty. People get credit for naming uncomfortable truths early.
5. Create decision triggers. Leaders define what would make them change course, before performance forces it.

These are not cultural statements. They are repeatable behaviours that reshape incentives through action.

Distributed Sensemaking The signals of change rarely arrive packaged nicely. They emerge across customer conversations online, cultural shifts, technologies and regulation. But when a single function has the responsibility to observe and interpret them, blind spots appear and multiply.

One of the fundamental beliefs in foresight is that cognitive diversity adds tremendous value to intelligence. Research by Hong and Page (2004) demonstrates mathematically that *'groups of diverse problem solvers can outperform groups of high-ability problem solvers'*. The advantage doesn't come from the average intelligence of the group, but from the variety of perspectives, heuristics and interpretive lenses applied to a problem. In futures intelligence, this suggests that when the interpretation of signals is distributed, that increases the range of possible future opportunities and solutions to problems an organization is able to meaningfully consider.[10]

Research on organizational sensemaking, specifically by Karl Weick, demonstrates that organizations not only process information, they interpret their environments through ongoing social interaction.[11] And when meaning is created collectively and not imposed hierarchically, there could be multiple interpretations held long enough to ensure ambiguity can be explored vs prematurely resolved.[12]

This means we should be inviting multiple opinions and points of view to interpret information in order to surface tensions, and welcoming competing explanations, not only to improve futures intelligence but also to address any conscious biases. However, we are not doing this to force consensus, we are inviting these perspectives to paint a fuller picture for everyone.

Decision Integration, Not Reporting One of the most common failure modes of foresight is that it produces reports rather than decisions. But if futures work is not linked to investment reviews, portfolio choices or strategic decisions — all these moments where trade-offs are made — then it will always be presented as supplementary material. A pre-read, merely for inspiration. Material that is interesting, informative but quickly dismissed and forgotten, because we don't take the opportunity to act on it.

Futures intelligence must shape agendas, decisions and governance checkpoints so that future considerations are unavoidable rather than optional. As we're exploring in this chapter, that means in many cases we need to create new, better systems rather than trying to fit foresight into a system that is already broken.

Learning Loops That Survive Failure Futures intelligence depends on learning, and learning implies being wrong — often and repeatedly.

Exploration is an activity that should be filled with experiments, brave ones at that. And these produce false signals, failed bets, misjudged trajectories. If we measure success for exploration activities in the same way we do for other organizational activities and the organization punishes failure instead of learning from it, then this is a sure way to teach people to avoid uncertainty and hide it, not to work with it.

Research on organizational ambidexterity by Charles O'Reilly and Michael Tushman shows that long-term performance depends on separating the evaluation of learning from the evaluation of short-term results.[13]

How to Measure Futures Intelligence Without Making It Performative

Senior leaders often ask, 'How do we know this is working?' Here are practical indicators that do not require complex scorecards.

Leading indicators:

- Percentage of major decisions that document explicit assumptions.
- Number of options in the portfolio that are designed to stay reversible.
- Frequency of trigger reviews in governance forums.
- Cross-functional participation in sensemaking, not just attendance.

Lagging indicators:

- Faster course correction when signals shift.
- Fewer late-stage strategy reversals under crisis pressure.
- Reduced overinvestment in a single assumed future.
- Stronger continuity of relevance, not just continuity of revenue.

The goal is not measurement for its own sake, but to make futures intelligence visible enough to manage and improve.

What This Looks Like in Practice

Organizations that successfully embed futures intelligence tend to make a small number of practical shifts.

- They move from episodic foresight actions to systematic sensing, interpreting and acting.
- They use future narratives and scenarios as a rehearsal to make decisions, not simply as nice storytelling to inspire.
- They prioritize (or at least, consider equally) early warning signals over backward-looking dashboards.
- They treat strategy as a set of evolving hypotheses rather than a fixed plan. (Very important in my experience!).

None of these require accurate prediction, but with disciplined attention and structural support implementing these practices will be a step-change in how future ready your organization will be.

A Concrete Example

A consumer services company ran quarterly trend reviews, but nothing changed. The foresight team produced strong analysis, yet business units treated it as optional.

They changed one thing: they embedded futures intelligence into an existing governance moment, the quarterly portfolio review.

Every product team had to bring:

- One external signal that could change demand.
- One assumption their roadmap depended on.
- One option they would preserve if that assumption weakened.
- One trigger that would force reallocation.

Within two cycles, the tone changed. Teams stopped debating whether the future mattered, and started debating what to do about it. Foresight did not 'win'. The decision process changed.

Closing the Decision Gap

At this point, I will assume that you have done the exercises in at least some of the Labs and have read Part I of the book. By now, at this stage in the book, the Decision Gap should definitely look different.

It should be clear that it is no longer just about individual courage or leadership style. Even with the best intent, these two are not going to be enough to produce the desired results, unless the organization itself has been re-designed to support decision-making under pressure and uncertainty.

Building futures intelligence and the enabling systems within the organization to interpret and really absorb what this intelligence shows within the decisions being made is how the Decision Gap begins to close. That doesn't happen by erasing uncertainty, but by making it usable, practicing with it and learning from it. And that requires Systems Learning.

12 Systems Learning and Organizational Maturity

Part II asked you to make choices under uncertainty.

You explored customers of the future, tested product relevance, confronted responsibility, mapped opportunity and stress-tested strategy. By the time you completed the Futures Strategy Canvas, you had turned foresight into structured decisions. You had done what most strategy processes avoid: commit before certainty arrives.

But a critical question remains: Do those decisions survive contact with the organization?

This chapter exists to close the Decision Gap at scale. The earlier chapters addressed the individual leader and the tools required to generate futures intelligence. Chapter 12 addresses whether the organization itself has the capacity to absorb that intelligence continuously rather than episodically.

Because the real gap is rarely between foresight and intention but tends to sit between foresight and institutionalization.

When Good Choices Become Isolated Events

It is not difficult to generate alignment in a workshop. It is much harder to ensure that alignment influences quarterly portfolio reviews, hiring decisions, capital allocation and incentive systems.

Many organizations treat foresight as an event. A project. A report. A strategic reset every few years.

The Strategic Futures Labs were deliberately designed to prevent that mindset. Each Lab connected foresight directly to a decision. But unless those decisions are integrated into the organization's operating rhythm, they remain isolated pockets of clarity.

From Choices to Capability means shifting the centre of gravity. The question becomes less about 'Did we run a good foresight process?' and more about 'Have we designed a system that continuously translates signals into commitment?'

And that shift requires Systems Learning.

Where the Future Actually Arrives

The future rarely enters an organization through a PowerPoint deck. It arrives at the edges, slowly and sporadically, not immediately visible to the untrained eye.

It starts to appear in frontline conversations with customers, in regulatory drafts circulating under the radar, in supply chain anomalies, in early dissatisfaction that metrics have not yet captured, in talent departures that feel anecdotal until they are not.

If those signals remain local, the core continues to operate as if nothing changed.

Systems Learning ensures that information flows from the edge to the centre before performance forces reaction. This builds on what I discussed about building futures intelligence at a team level in Chapter 11.

Figure 12.1 illustrates how signals driven by external forces (STEEP) first surface at the edges of the organization, often in fragmented and informal ways. These signals are captured and brought into structured sensemaking forums, where they are interpreted and tested against existing assumptions. From there, the most relevant foresight is elevated into governance discussions, shaping strategic review and ultimately influencing resource allocation and action.

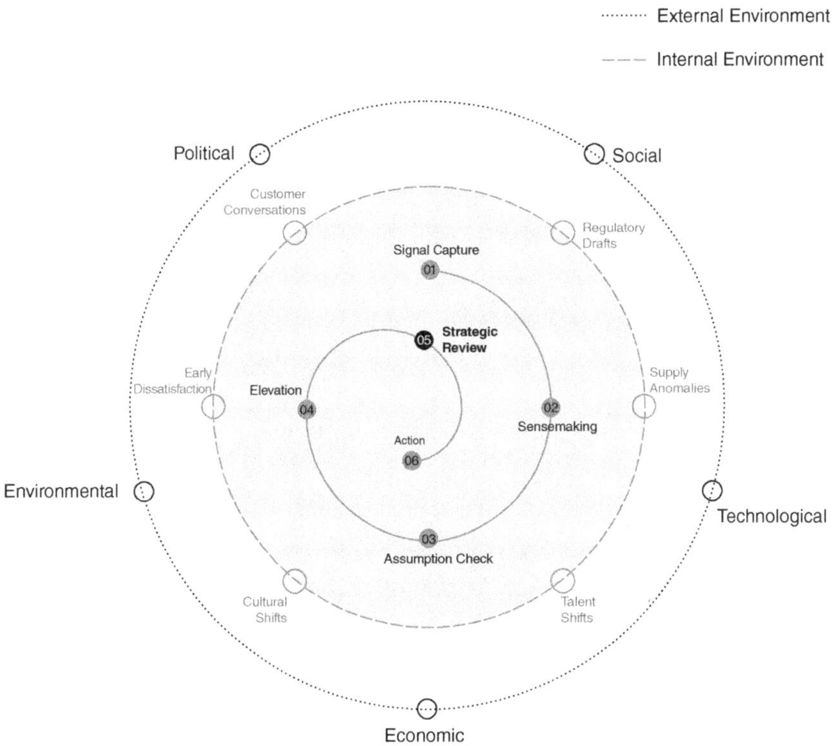

Figure 12.1 Edge-to-core Feedback Flow.

The intent should not be to centralize all information, but to ensure that weak signals feed into futures intelligence and travel far enough to influence decisions before performance forces a reactive response.

To design this flow, you need to clearly define the pathways and roles, and these are often a cross-department responsibility:

- Who is responsible for interpreting emerging signals?
- How frequently are they surfaced beyond their original function and in what form — an isolated signal or they fed the futures intelligence?
- In which governance moment do they influence decisions?

Without those pathways, futures intelligence remains interesting but inconsequential.

Moving Beyond Projects

A common trap in corporate foresight is treating uncertainty as a periodic disruption that requires special treatment. That logic assumes that stability is the norm and ambiguity is an interruption.

The reality is more continuous.

Volatility, technological acceleration, geopolitical fragmentation, regulatory complexity and shifting social expectations are not episodic. They are structural conditions, as we have seen.

Organizations that mature stop running 'future projects' and begin building adaptive habits.

The Futures Strategy Canvas helps here. It was never meant to be a static artifact. It functions as a memory structure that records assumptions, options, no-regret actions, conditional bets and triggers. When revisited rhythmically, it preserves coherence while allowing movement.

This is what moves foresight from presentation material to infrastructure.

What Organizational Maturity Really Means

Maturity in this context is not about age, scale or industry. It is about how well an organization can adjust without losing direction.

A mature organization can:

- Articulate the assumptions behind its strategy.
- Define conditions under which it would revise them.
- Reallocate resources before decline becomes irreversible.
- Hold multiple plausible futures in conversation without paralysis.
- Treat legitimacy and system contribution as performance variables.

Traditional linear planning often equated maturity with control and precision. The environment in which we now operate rewards adaptability with discipline instead.

The difference becomes visible in behaviour.

In less mature systems, strategy discussions default to historical performance data and demand extrapolated certainty. In more mature systems, leaders ask what must remain true and what could invalidate current commitments. Assumptions are written down rather than implied.

Over time, there is less theatre, more clarity and fewer surprise crises.

The Operating Model of Systems Learning

Systems Learning depends on a rhythm rather than intensity (Figure 12.2).

Signals are noticed and interpreted collectively, assumptions are surfaced before commitments are locked in, decisions are made conditionally, triggers are predefined conditions that signal when to adjust decisions, reducing reliance on subjective judgement or debate, governance forums revisit bets before they fail rather than after.

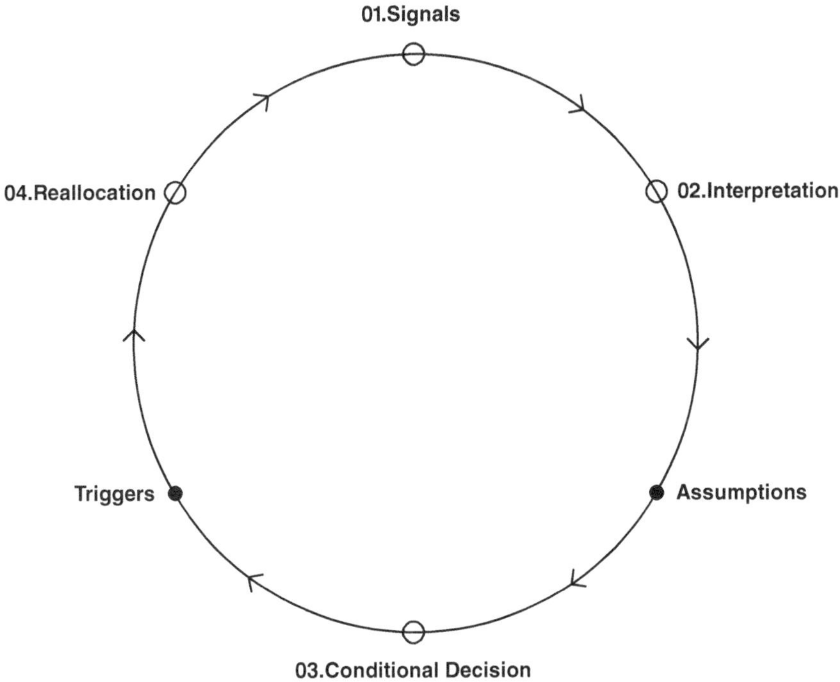

Figure 12.2 The Systems Learning Cycle.

When this cycle functions reliably, the organization stops oscillating between complacency and panic.

This rhythm transforms the Strategic Futures Labs from exercises into useful and permanent decision lenses.

Scaling the Futures Playbook

Chapter 9 helped you construct your Futures Playbook. Scaling it requires deliberate integration.

Implementation rarely begins enterprise-wide. It usually begins where governance is active and then trickles down to other areas of the business. Try this:

- Start with one portfolio review and embed assumption tracking.
- Use the Futures Strategy Canvas in one business unit to document conditional bets.
- Incorporate trigger discussions into one executive meeting.
- Reward one early adjustment that resulted from signal recognition rather than performance decline.

These shifts may feel incremental, but over time they compound into a capability.

The goal is coherence across teams. When different units speak the same language of assumptions, options and triggers, alignment increases naturally.

This is how futures thinking stops being 'owned' by a single function and becomes a shared discipline.

The Leadership Inflection Point

Leadership ultimately determines whether Systems Learning strengthens or weakens.

If leaders demand precise forecasts where precision is impossible, teams will manufacture certainty. If leaders equate changing course with inconsistency, people will delay adjustments. If leaders treat foresight as peripheral, it will remain peripheral.

Adaptive organizations are shaped by leaders who:

- Ask for assumptions before approving commitments.
- Revisit decisions openly when signals shift.
- Protect early-stage options long enough for them to mature.
- Legitimize uncertainty as a working condition.
- Align incentives with long-term relevance rather than short-term stability alone.

Over time, these behaviours reshape norms. People begin escalating weak signals earlier, conversations widen instead of narrowing under pressure, and this is how maturity compounds.

From Linear Plans to Living Strategy

Earlier chapters demonstrated how linear thinking breaks in non-linear environments. This chapter closes the loop. Revisit Chapter 1 if you still need convincing of the business case for properly embedded futures thinking — or if you are seeking research to support your perspective when discussing its necessity with others on your leadership team.

The shift from choices to capability is the shift from episodic foresight to embedded adaptation.

In linear models, strategy is periodically redesigned. But as we've seen, linear models are no longer fit for the world in which we live. In more mature systems, strategy is continuously refined, assumptions are alive, triggers are visible, reallocation is deliberate rather than reactive. These are crucial approaches in the BANI world that now exists where uncertainty abounds.

Advanced organizations that reach this stage do not eliminate uncertainty — they make a much more strategically valuable choice — they design for it.

The Decision Gap narrows because futures intelligence now has a structural pathway to influence commitment.

The Real Measure of Progress

If you want to know whether Systems Learning is taking root, observe what happens when uncertainty increases.

Does the organization tighten and demand more proof?

Or does it slow down slightly, revisit assumptions and act intentionally?

That difference reveals maturity more clearly than any slide or declaration.

When futures intelligence is embedded, better decisions no longer rely on extraordinary effort from individual leaders. They are supported by cadence, infrastructure and aligned incentives.

That is how foresight stops being an initiative and becomes capability.

And that is how the organization remains adaptive long after the workshop energy fades.

Afterword

I have known Joana for years, and what has always stood out to me is her quiet obsession with one of the most overlooked problems in business today, the gap between foresight and action. We are living in a time where leaders are flooded with trends, scenarios, and signals about the future, yet very few know how to translate that awareness into meaningful decisions, and that is exactly where this book does its most important work.

From Foresight to Action tackles what I often speak about in my own work, that the future is not about what you know, it is about how you behave. Joana brings this to life in a practical and grounded way, showing that foresight only becomes valuable when it shapes real choices, when it influences where you commit, where you hold back, and how you move under uncertainty. This is where most organizations struggle, and it is where Joana has spent years paying attention, refining her thinking, and building a framework that actually works in the real world.

What I appreciate most is that this is not theory dressed up as strategy, it is a playbook designed for leaders who are under pressure to decide without perfect information. Her Strategic Futures Labs create the kind of tension and trade-offs that mirror reality, and in doing so, they help build the one capability that matters most in the years ahead, adaptability.

Congratulations, Joana, this is a timely and necessary piece of work. If you are in a leadership role and want to become more decisive, more relevant and more prepared for what is coming, this is a book worth your time.

—*John Sanei*

Futurist and Global Keynote Speaker

About the Author

Joana Lenkova is a distinguished Bulgarian-British strategist and professional futurist with over 20 years of international experience, having held high-profile roles at the LEGO Group, The Walt Disney Company, AB InBev and Societe Generale. She is currently the Director of Cultural and Futures Intelligence at the LEGO Group.

In 2019, Joana founded Futures Forward Ltd, a London-based consultancy known for guiding global brands, governmental institutions and NGOs toward future skills and opportunities. Her firm specializes in leveraging cutting-edge foresight and robust strategic frameworks to prepare organizations for dynamic market shifts, technological advancements and their implication on needs and societal values.

Through her work, she leads the development of advanced foresight capabilities, enhancing brand strategies with valuable futures intelligence that drives sustainable growth and business adaptability.

By embedding foresight and innovation into their core strategic processes, she enhances decision-making and competitive edge. Her work synthesizes complex data and emerging signals into actionable foresight, helping organizations navigate and proactively shape an ever-changing global landscape.

An alumna of Saïd Business School, University of Oxford, Joana is a respected voice in the innovation, strategy and foresight community, actively contributing to global forums on emerging trends, foresight capability building and strategic planning. Her foresight, known for its depth and applicability, addresses today's pressing business challenges with a forward-looking perspective.

Joana is also an Advisory Board member of the Strategic Consortium of Intelligence Professionals (SCIP), a non-profit community that is the world's largest intelligence association. SCIP has over 25,000 individual members across 120 countries. All opinions are her own.

Conclusion: Designing Your Intentional Future

The Next Step Forward: Stay Curious, Stay Adaptive

Across the Strategic Futures Labs in this book, you have worked with foresight in its proper role: as data about external change — trends, signals, scenarios — and turned it into futures intelligence: insight interpreted in context. Yet this is precisely the moment where many organizations stall.

They see more clearly, but act no differently.

The gap between what leaders can now see and what they are willing to commit to is the Decision Gap as we have discussed. But the difference between the person who first opened this book and the person you are now is that you have tools and language to enable you to effectively bridge this gap.

Closing the Decision Gap is not one decision, it's a system of decisions.

The Labs gave you practice, Chapter 9 gave you the Canvas. But what makes this durable is repetition: sensing, choosing, testing, adjusting. That is Systems Learning, and it is what turns futures thinking from an isolated event into maturity.

Why Strategies Fail After Foresight

When organizations fail to act on futures intelligence, the barrier is rarely technical. It is structural and behavioural, as I've outlined.

Typically, four patterns show up: decision-making slows under uncertainty, experimentation is encouraged rhetorically but punished structurally, learning loops are weak or absent, governance mechanisms prioritize protecting the past over adapting to change. This pattern is not anecdotal.

As a reminder, research by René Rohrbeck demonstrates a strong correlation between future preparedness and long-term firm performance, but only when foresight is embedded into decision-making processes, rather than isolated as a specialized function.[1] I repeat this here because this insight is the key to building a more robust, adaptive organization.

In other words, foresight does not fail because it is speculative. It fails because organizations are not designed to act on what it reveals. Before I leave you, let's explore what Systems Learning looks like when you use the tools you've uncovered through the Labs.

A Short Example of Systems Learning

A leadership team noticed early signals that customer trust was shifting, but revenue was still strong. In the past, they would have waited for the numbers to force action.

This time, they used the Futures Strategy Canvas.

They wrote the assumptions, defined triggers and made one option investment that kept flexibility open. Six months later, regulation tightened faster than expected. But they did not panic. They activated the trigger plan they had already agreed to.

It sounds like a brilliant execution, perhaps too good to be true, but it can be achieved with practice. You will not get every decision right. That is part of life. But you will make decisions with greater clarity than if you set this book aside and go back to business as usual.

From Insight to Commitment: The Role of the Futures Strategy Canvas

You now have a way to work with complexity without oversimplifying it. A way to explore futures without pretending to predict them. A way to test strategy before reality does. And a way to design decisions that can evolve over time.

Most importantly, you have a language — shared, practical and grounded — for talking about uncertainty without fear or false confidence. The future will continue to surprise you. That will not change. What can change is how prepared you are to respond when it does.

If you want a practical starting point, do this on Monday morning:

Pick one decision that matters this quarter, write the assumptions, then define one option and set one trigger. Then repeat.

That is how organizations become future-ready. Not through one dramatic innovation, but through deliberate, disciplined, repeated choice. This is how to begin leading beyond the edge of certainty. We all know, on some level at least, that one of the only certainties in the world as I write this is that uncertainty abounds. This is an uncomfortable truth to face. But you have now sat with uncomfortable truths in the Labs. You have faced them — and you must if you are to lead in an increasingly uncertain world.

A Final Question

As you close this book, one question remains, and it is not a strategic one. It is actually a deliberate choice. When the future challenges your assumptions, will you protect what exists or design what comes next?

That answer, repeated over time, is what shapes organizations. And futures. If your answer is to 'design what comes next' you are taking steps to move from foresight to action. You are not simply seeing change on the horizon. You are acting to respond to that change in a way calmly using the foresight available to you. And when you embed systems in your organization that encourage others to do the same, you are building resilience. You are developing Systems Learning. Organizations that learn and act in this way are not waiting for the future to arrive. They are creating the conditions for the future they want to see. With what you've learned in this book, you too can shape your own future.

Notes

Introduction

1. World Economic Forum. (2026). *The Global Risks Report 2026*, 21st Edition. https://www.weforum.org/publications/global-risks-report-2026 (accessed 27 March 2026).
2. Tetlock, P.E. (2005). *Expert Political Judgment: How Good Is It? How Can We Know?* Princeton: Princeton University Press.
3. Tetlock, P.E. and Gardner, D. (2015). *Superforecasting: The Art and Science of Prediction*. New York: Crown.

Chapter 1

1. Wienefoet, T. (2025). Strategic foresight: how CFOs turn uncertainty into advantage – part 1 of 3. https://fpa-trends.com/article/strategic-foresight-how-cfos-turn-uncertainty-advantage-part-1-3 (accessed 27 March 2026). Cascio, J. (2020). 'Facing the age of chaos', *Medium*, 29 April. https://medium.com/@cascio/facing-the-age-of-chaos-b00687b1f51d (accessed 25 April 2026).
2. Ferganani, A. (2022). Corporate foresight: a new frontier for strategy and management. *Academy of Management Perspectives* 36(2). https://doi.org/10.5465/amp.2018.0178.
3. Bańbura, M., Giannone, D., and Reichlin, L. (2011). Nowcasting. In: *The Oxford Handbook of Economic Forecasting* (eds. M.P. Clements and D.F. Hendry). Oxford: Oxford University Press.

4. Rohrbeck, R. and Kum, M.E. (2018). Corporate foresight and its impact on firm performance: A longitudinal analysis. *Technological Forecasting and Social Change* 129(4): 105–116. https://doi.org/10.1016/j.techfore.2017.12.013.
5. Ibid.
6. Ibid.
7. Ibid.
8. Rohrbeck, R. and Schwarz, J.O. (2013). The value contribution of strategic foresight: insights from an empirical study of large European companies. *Technological Forecasting and Social Change* 80(8): 1593–1606. https://doi.org/10.1016/j.techfore.2013.01.004.
9. Wienefoet, Strategic foresight, part 1.
10. Rohrbeck and Schwarz, The value contribution of strategic foresight.
11. Wienefoet, Strategic foresight, part 1.
12. Bereznoy, A. (2017). Corporate foresight in multinational business strategies. *Foresight and STI Governance* 11(1): 9–22. https://foresight-journal.hse.ru/article/view/19336 (accessed 25 April 2026).
13. Backler, W., Iny, A., D'Intino, N. et al. (2025). Navigating the future with strategic foresight. BCG. https://www.bcg.com/publications/2025/navigating-the-future-with-strategic-foresight (accessed 27 March 2026).
14. Rohrbeck and Kum, Corporate foresight and its impact on firm performance.
15. Ibid.
16. Bereznoy, Corporate foresight in multinational business strategies.
17. Rohrbeck and Schwarz, The value contribution of strategic foresight.
18. Ibid.
19. Wienefoet, Strategic foresight, part 1.
20. Sen, A. (2024). The silent killer: why your CFO's lack of strategic thinking is threatening your business. https://fifthchrome.com/the-silent-killer-cfo-lack-of-strategic-thinking-threatening-business (accessed 27 March 2026).
21. Wienefoet, T. (2025). Strategic foresight for CFOs: understanding the future before it happens – part 2 of 3. https://fpa-trends.com/article/strategic-foresight-understanding-future-part-2-3 (accessed 27 March 2026).
22. Rohrbeck and Kum, Corporate foresight and its impact on firm performance.
23. Kennedy, J.F. (1962). Annual message to the Congress on the State of the Union, 11 January. Miller Center, University of Virginia. https://millercenter.org/the-presidency/presidential-speeches/january-11-1962-state-union-address (accessed 25 April 2026).

24. CNBC. (2025). Novo Nordisk's 'long game' on weight-loss drugs sparks hope in science, but the Street is impatient. CNBC, 30 December. https://www.cnbc.com/2025/12/30/novo-nordisk-beyond-weight-loss-has-investors-wary-scientists-hopeful.html (accessed 25 April 2026).
25. Rohrbeck, R. and Gemünden, H.G. (2011). Corporate foresight: its three roles in enhancing the innovation capacity of a firm. *Technological Forecasting and Social Change* 78(2): 231–243. https://doi.org/10.1016/j.techfore.2010.06.019.
26. Wack, P. (1985). Scenarios: uncharted waters ahead. *Harvard Business Review* 63(5): 73–89; Wilkinson, A. and Kupers, R. (2013). Living in the futures. *Harvard Business Review* 91(5): 118–127.
27. Wienefoet, Strategic foresight, part 2.
28. de Geus, A. (1997). *The Living Company: Habits for Survival in a Turbulent Business Environment.* Boston: Harvard Business School Press.

Chapter 2

1. *Peloton Interactive (PTON) Statistics & Valuation.* https://stockanalysis.com/stocks/pton/statistics (accessed 26 March 2026). Levy, A. (2024). How much money you'd have lost if you invested at Peloton's IPO. *CNBC*, 3 May. https://www.cnbc.com/2024/05/03/how-much-money-youd-have-lost-if-you-invested-at-pelotons-ipo.html (accessed 26 April 2026); Whitten, S. (2022). Peloton to pause production of its bikes and treadmills as demand wanes. *CNBC*, 20 January. https://www.cnbc.com/2022/01/20/peloton-to-pause-production-of-its-bikes-treadmills-as-demand-wanes.html (accessed 26 April 2026).
2. Whitten, S. (2022). Peloton shares jump as company announces price hikes for some products. *CNBC*, 12 August. https://www.cnbc.com/2022/08/12/peloton-shares-jump-as-company-announces-price-hikes-for-some-products.html (accessed 26 April 2026).
3. Danh, V. (2021). Peloton's vertical integration and explosive growth in 2020. *Medium.* https://danh-tu-vic.medium.com/pelotons-vertical-integration-and-explosive-growth-in-2020-333e3ea98526 (accessed 26 March 2026).
4. Business of Apps. (2026). Health & Fitness App Report 2026. https://www.businessofapps.com/data/health-fitness-app-report/ (accessed 26 April 2026).
5. Sun Tzu. (2002). *The Art of War*, trans. L. Giles. Mineola, NY: Dover Publications.

6. Christensen, C.M. (1997). *The Innovator's Dilemma: When New Technologies Cause Great Firms to Fail.* Boston: Harvard Business School Press.
7. Tushman, M.L. and O'Reilly, C.A. (1996). Ambidextrous organizations: managing evolutionary and revolutionary change. *California Management Review* 38(4): 8–30.
8. O'Reilly, C.A. and Tushman, M.L. (2013). Organizational ambidexterity: past, present, and future. *Academy of Management Perspectives* 27(4): 324–338.
9. Rohrbeck, R. and Schwarz, J.O. (2013). The value contribution of strategic foresight: insights from an empirical study of large European companies. *Technological Forecasting and Social Change* 80(8): 1593–1606.
10. de Geus, A. (1997). The living company. *Harvard Business Review* 75(2): 51+. *Gale Academic OneFile*, link.gale.com/apps/doc/A19698724/AONE?u=anon~1439eb91&sid=googleScholar&xid=d16c9d98 (accessed 26 March 2026).
11. Zenger, T. (2013). What is the theory of your firm? *Harvard Business Review* 91(6): 72–78. https://hbr.org/2013/06/what-is-the-theory-of-your-firm (accessed 26 April 2026).
12. Mayer, C. and Roche, B. (eds.) (2021). *Putting Purpose into Practice: The Economics of Mutuality*. Oxford: Oxford University Press.

Chapter 3

1. Snowden, D.J. and Boone, M.E. (2007). A leader's framework for decision making. *Harvard Business Review* 85(11): 68–76. https://hbr.org/2007/11/a-leaders-framework-for-decision-making.
2. Meadows, D. (2008). *Thinking in Systems. A Primer.* White River Junction, VT: Chelsea Green Publishing.
3. Spitz, R. (2024). *Disrupt with Impact: Achieve Business Success in an Unpredictable World.* London: Kogan Page.
4. Einstein, B. (2025). Understanding how to use the ladder of inference. https://online.hbs.edu/blog/post/ladder-of-inference (accessed 29 March 2026); Argyris, C. (1990). *Overcoming Organizational Defenses: Facilitating Organizational Learning*. Boston: Allyn & Bacon.
5. The Systems Thinker. (2016). The ladder of inference. https://thesystemsthinker.com/the-ladder-of-inference (accessed 29 March 2026).
6. Kahneman, D. (2011). *Thinking, Fast and Slow.* New York: Farrar, Straus and Giroux.

7. Samuelson, W. and Zeckhauser, R. (1988). Status quo bias in decision making. *Journal of Risk and Uncertainty* 1(1): 7–59. https://doi.org/10.1007/BF00055564.
8. Confirmation bias: Nickerson, R.S. (1998). Confirmation bias: a ubiquitous phenomenon in many guises. *Review of General Psychology* 2(2): 175–220.
9. Kahneman, D. and Tversky, A. (1979). Prospect theory: an analysis of decision under risk. *Econometrica* 47(2): 263–291. https://doi.org/10.2307/1914185.
10. Denrell, J. (2003). Vicarious learning, undersampling of failure, and the myths of management. *Organization Science* 14(3): 227–243.
11. Arkes, H.R. and Blumer, C. (1985). The psychology of sunk cost. *Organizational Behavior and Human Decision Processes* 35(1): 124–140. https://doi.org/10.1016/0749-5978(85)90049-4; Staw, B.M. (1976). Knee-deep in the big muddy: a study of escalating commitment to a chosen course of action. *Organizational Behavior and Human Performance* 16(1): 27–44. https://doi.org/10.1016/0030-5073(76)90005-2.
12. Meadows, D. (2008). *Thinking in Systems.*
13. Senge, P.M. (1990). *The Fifth Discipline: The Art and Practice of the Learning Organization.* New York: Doubleday.
14. Inayatullah, S. (1998). Causal layered analysis: poststructuralism as method. *Futures* 30(8): 815–829. https://doi.org/10.1016/S0016-3287(98)00086-X.
15. Meadows D. (2008). *Thinking in Systems.*
16. Tetlock, P.E. and Gardner, D. (2015). *Superforecasting: The Art and Science of Prediction.* New York: Crown.
17. Miller, R. (ed.) (2018). *Transforming the Future: Anticipation in the 21st Century.* Paris: UNESCO/Routledge. https://doi.org/10.4324/9781351048002.

Chapter 4

1. Christensen, C.M., Hall, T., Dillon, K., and Duncan, D.S. (2016). *Competing Against Luck: The Story of Innovation and Customer Choice.* New York: HarperBusiness.
2. Ulwick, A.W. (2002). Turn customer input into innovation. *Harvard Business Review* 80(1): 91–97. https://hbr.org/2002/01/turn-customer-input-into-innovation.

3. Maslow, A.H. (1943). A theory of human motivation. *Psychological Review* 50(4): 370–396. https://doi.org/10.1037/h0054346.
4. Max-Neef, M.A. (1991). *Human Scale Development: Conception, Application and Further Reflections*. New York: The Apex Press.
5. Turkle, S. (2011). *Alone Together: Why We Expect More from Technology and Less from Each Other*. New York: Basic Books.
6. Zuboff, S. (2019). *The Age of Surveillance Capitalism: The Fight for a Human Future at the New Frontier of Power*. New York: PublicAffairs.
7. The Futures School. (2020). The 3 environments of foresight, March. https://tfsx.com/2020/03/the-3-environments-of-foresight/ (accessed 26 April 2026).
8. Chapman, C.N. and Milham, R.P. (2006). The personas' new clothes: methodological and practical arguments against a popular method. *Proceedings of the Human Factors and Ergonomics Society Annual Meeting* 50(5): 634–636. https://doi.org/10.1177/154193120605000503.
9. Maslow, A.H. (1943). A theory of human motivation. *Psychological Review* 50(4): 370–396. https://doi.org/10.1037/h0054346.
10. Sen, A. (1999). *Development as Freedom*. Oxford: Oxford University Press.
11. Nussbaum, M.C. (2000). *Women and Human Development: The Capabilities Approach*. Cambridge: Cambridge University Press.
12. Deci, E.L. and Ryan, R.M. (1985). *Intrinsic Motivation and Self-Determination in Human Behavior*. New York: Plenum.
13. Max-Neef, *Human Scale Development*.
14. Zuboff, *The Age of Surveillance Capitalism*.

Chapter 5

1. McGrath, R.G. (2013). *The End of Competitive Advantage: How to Keep Your Strategy Moving as Fast as Your Business*. Boston: Harvard Business Review Press.
2. Henderson, B.D. (1970). *The Product Portfolio*. Boston: Boston Consulting Group (BCG Perspectives).
3. Christensen, C.M., Hall, T., Dillon, K., and Duncan, D.S. (2016). *Competing Against Luck: The Story of Innovation and Customer Choice*. New York: HarperBusiness.

4. Guha, A., Grewal, D., Kopalle, P.K., et al. (2021). How artificial intelligence will affect the future of retailing. *Journal of Retailing* 97(1): 28–41. https://doi.org/10.1016/j.jretai.2021.01.005.
5. Kellogg, K., Valentine, M.A., and Christin, A. (2020). Algorithms at work. *Academy of Management Annals* 14(1): 366–410.
6. Ryan, R.M. and Deci, E.L. (2000). Self-determination theory and the facilitation of intrinsic motivation, social development, and well-being. *American Psychologist* 55(1): 68–78. https://doi.org/10.1037/0003-066X.55.1.68.
7. Max-Neef, M.A. (1991). *Human Scale Development: Conception, Application and Further Reflections*. New York: The Apex Press.
8. Nielsen, J. (2010). Mental models. Nielsen Norman Group, 17 October. https://www.nngroup.com/articles/mental-models/ (accessed 29 March 2026).
9. Max-Neef, *Human Scale Development*.
10. Meadows, D. (2008). *Thinking in Systems*. New York: Chelsea Green Publishing.
11. Schoemaker, P.J.H. (1995). Scenario planning: a tool for strategic thinking. *Sloan Management Review* 36(2): 25–40. https://sloanreview.mit.edu/article/scenario planning-a-tool-for-strategic-thinking (accessed 27 April 2026).

Chapter 6

1. The Futures School. (n.d.). Probability/Impact Matrix Mural Template. https://tfsx.com/shop/probability-impact-matrix-mural-template (accessed 26 April 2026).

Chapter 7

1. Baghai, M., Coley, S., and White, D. (1999). *The Alchemy of Growth: Practical Insights for Building the Enduring Enterprise*. Cambridge, MA: Perseus Publishing.

Chapter 8

1. van der Heijden, K. (2005). *Scenarios: The Art of Strategic Conversation*. Chichester: John Wiley & Sons.

Chapter 10

1. Bazerman, M. and Moore, D. (2013). *Judgment in Managerial Decision Making*, 8th ed. Wiley.
2. APA Dictionary of Psychology. (2018). 'Heuristic'. https://dictionary.apa.org/heuristic (accessed 30 March 2026).
3. Sarinopoulos, I., Grupe, D.W., Mackiewicz, K.L. et al. (2010). Uncertainty during anticipation modulates neural responses to aversion in human insula and amygdala. *Cerebral Cortex* 20(4): 929–940.
4. Kahneman, D. and Tversky, A. (1979). Prospect theory: an analysis of decision under risk. *Econometrica* 47(2): 263–291. https://doi.org/10.2307/1914185.
5. Tetlock, P.E. and Gardner, D. (2015). *Superforecasting: The Art and Science of Prediction*. Crown.
6. Johns, G. (2006). The essential impact of context on organizational behavior. *Academy of Management Review* 31(2): 386–408.

Chapter 11

1. Schwarz, J.O., Rohrbeck, R. and Wach, B. (2020). Corporate foresight as a microfoundation of dynamic capabilities. *Futures & Foresight Science* 2(2): e28. https://doi.org/10.1002/ffo2.28.
2. Rohrbeck, R. and Kum, M.E. (2018). Corporate foresight and its impact on firm performance: a longitudinal analysis. *Technological Forecasting and Social Change* 129: 105–116. https://doi.org/10.1016/j.techfore.2017.12.013; Schwarz, J.O., Rohrbeck, R., and Wach, B. (2020). Corporate foresight as a microfoundation of dynamic capabilities. *Futures & Foresight Science* 2(2): e28. https://doi.org/10.1002/ffo2.28.
3. Rohrbeck, R. and Schwarz, J.O. (2013). The value contribution of strategic foresight. *Technological Forecasting and Social Change* 80(8): 1593–1606.
4. Rohrbeck and Kum, Corporate foresight and its impact on firm performance.
5. Gordon, A.V., Ramic, M., Rohrbeck, R. et al. (2020). 50 years of corporate and organizational foresight. *Technological Forecasting and Social Change* 154: 119966. https://doi.org/10.1016/j.techfore.2020.119966.
6. Rohrbeck, R. and Gemünden, H.G. (2011). Corporate foresight: its three roles in enhancing the innovation capacity of a firm. *Technological Forecasting and Social Change* 78(2): 231–243.

7. Miller, R. (ed.) (2018). *Transforming the Future: Anticipation in the 21st Century*. Paris: UNESCO/Routledge. https://doi.org/10.4324/9781351048002.
8. Staw, B.M., Sandelands, L.E., and Dutton, J.E. (1981). Threat-rigidity effects in organizational behavior: a multilevel analysis. *Administrative Science Quarterly* 26(4): 501–524.
9. Højland, J. and Rohrbeck, R. (2018). The role of corporate foresight in exploring new markets – evidence from 3 case studies in the BOP markets. *Technology Analysis & Strategic Management* 30(6): 734–746. https://doi.org/10.1080/09537325.2017.1337887.
10. Hong, L. and Page, S.E. (2004). Groups of diverse problem solvers can outperform groups of high-ability problem solvers. *Proceedings of the National Academy of Sciences* 101 (46): 16385–16389. https://www.pnas.org/doi/full/10.1073/pnas.0403723101 (accessed 31 March 2026).
11. Weick, K.E. (1995). *Sensemaking in Organizations*. Sage Publications. https://www.researchgate.net/publication/257397559_Sensemaking_in_organizations_by_Karl_E_Weick_Thousand_Oaks_CA_Sage_Publications_1995_231_pp (accessed 31 March 2026).
12. Weick, *Sensemaking in Organizations*.
13. O'Reilly III, C.A. and Tushman, M.L. (2021). *Lead and Disrupt: How to Solve the Innovator's Dilemma*, 2nd ed. Stanford, CA: Stanford Business Books.

Conclusion

1. Rohrbeck, R. and Kum, M.E. (2018). Corporate foresight and its impact on firm performance: A longitudinal analysis. *Technological Forecasting and Social Change* 129(4): 105–116.

Index